A
MEDITATIVE
COMMENTARY
ON THE
NEW TESTAMENT

HEBREWS & JAMES: BROTHER JESUS

HEBREWS & JAMES: BROTHER JESUS

By Gary Holloway

LEAFWOOD
PUBLISHERS

HEBREWS & JAMES: BROTHER JESUS
Published by Leafwood Publishers

Copyright 2007 by Gary Holloway

ISBN 978-0-89112-505-1
Printed in the United States of America

Cover design by Greg Jackson, Jackson Design Co., llc

For information contact:
Leafwood Publishers, Abilene, Texas
1-877-816-4455 toll free
www.leafwoodpublishers.com

07 08 09 10 11 12 / 7 6 5 4 3 2 1

To Mark Black, the friend closer than a brother

C O N T E N T S

JAMES: THE WISDOM OF JESUS

MEDITATIONS

INTRODUCTION

HEARING GOD IN SCRIPTURE

Many good commentaries, guides, and workbooks exist on the various books of the Bible. How is this series different? It is not intended to answer all your scholarly questions about the Bible, or even make you an expert in the details of Scripture. Instead, this series is designed to help you hear the voice of God for your everyday life. It is a guide to meditation on the Bible, meditation that will allow the Bible to transform you.

We read in many ways. We might scan the newspaper for information, read a map for location, read a novel for pleasure, or read a textbook to pass a test. These are all good ways to read, depending on our circumstances.

A young soldier far away from home who receives a letter from his wife reads in yet another way. He might scan the letter quickly at first for news and information. But his longing for his beloved causes him to read the letter again and again, hearing her sweet voice in every line. He slowly treasures each word of this precious letter.

BIBLE STUDY

So also, there are many good ways to read the Bible, depending on our circumstances. Bible study is absolutely necessary for our life with God. We rightly study the Bible for information. We ask, "Who wrote this?" "When was it written?" "Who were the original readers?"

"How do these words apply to me?" More importantly, we want information about God. Who is he? What does he think of me? What does he want from me?

There is no substitute for this kind of close, dedicated Bible study. We must know what the Bible says to know our standing with God. We therefore read the Bible to discover true doctrine or teaching. But some in their emphasis on the authority and inspiration of the Bible have forgotten that Bible study is not an end in itself. We want to know God through Scripture. We want to have a relationship with the Teacher, not just the teachings.

Jesus tells some of God's people in his day, "You diligently study the Scriptures because you think that by them you possess eternal life. These are the Scriptures that testify about me, yet you refuse to come to me to have life" (John 5:39-40). He's not telling them to study their Bibles less, but he is reminding them of the deeper purpose of Bible study—to draw us to God through Jesus. Bible study is a means, not an end.

Yet the way many of us have learned to study the Bible may actually get in the way of hearing God. "Bible study" may sound a lot like schoolwork, and many of us were happy to get out of school. "Bible study" may call to mind pictures of intellectuals surrounded by books in Greek and Hebrew, pondering meanings too deep for ordinary people. The method of Bible study that has been popular for some time focuses on the strangeness of the Bible. It was written long ago, far away, and in languages we cannot read. There is a huge gap between us and the original readers of the Bible, a gap that can only be bridged by scholars, not by average folk.

There is some truth and some value in that "scholarly" method. It is true that the Bible was not written originally to us. Knowing ancient languages and customs can at times help us understand the Bible better. However, one unintended result of this approach is to make the Bible distant from the people of God. We may come to think that we can only hear God indirectly through Scripture, that his word must be filtered through scholars. We may even think that deep Bible study is a matter of mastering obscure information about the Bible.

MEDITATION

But we read the Bible for more than information. By studying it, we experience transformation, the mysterious process of God at work in us. Through his loving words, God is calling us to life with him. He is forming us into the image of his Son.

Reading the Bible is not like reading other books. We are not simply trying to learn information or master material. Instead, we want to stand under the authority of Scripture and let God master us. While we read the Bible, it reads us, opening the depths of our being to the overpowering love of God. "For the word of God is living and active. Sharper than any double-edged sword, it penetrates even to dividing soul and spirit, joints and marrow; it judges the thoughts and attitudes of the heart. Nothing in all creation is hidden from God's sight. Everything is uncovered and laid bare before the eyes of him to whom we must give account" (Hebrews 4:12-13).

Opening our hearts to the word of God is meditation. Although this way of reading the Bible may be new to some, it has a long heritage among God's people. The Psalmist joyously meditates on the words of God (Psalm 1:2; 39:3; 119:15, 23, 27, 48, 78, 97, 99, 148). Meditation is taking the words of Scripture to heart and letting them ask questions of us. It is slowly chewing over a text, listening closely, reading God's message of love to us over and over. This is not a simple, easy, or naïve reading of Scripture, but a process that takes time, dedication, and practice on our part.

There are many ways to meditate on the Bible. One is praying the Scriptures. Prayer and Bible study really cannot be separated. One way of praying the Bible is to make the words of a text your prayer. Obviously, the prayer texts of Scripture, especially the Psalms, lend themselves to this. "The Lord is my shepherd" has been the prayer of many hearts.

However, it is proper and helpful to turn the words of the Bible into prayers. Commands from God can become prayers. "You shall have no other gods before me" (Exodus 20:3) can be prayed, "Lord, keep me from anything that takes your place in my heart." Stories can be prayed. Jesus heals a man born blind (John 9), and so we pray, "Lord Jesus open my eyes to who you truly are." Even the promises of the Bible become prayers. "Never will I leave you; never will I forsake you" (Deuteronomy 31:6; Hebrews 13:5) becomes "God help me know that you promise that you are always with me and so live my life without fear."

Obviously, there are many helpful ways of hearing the voice of God in Scripture. Again, the purpose of Bible reading and study is not to know more about the Bible, much less to pride ourselves as experts on Scripture. Instead, we read to hear the voice of our Beloved. We listen for a word of God for us.

Holy Reading

This commentary reflects one ancient way of meditation and praying the Scriptures known as lectio divina or holy reading. This method assumes that God wants to speak to us directly in the Bible, that the passage we are reading is God's word to us right now. The writers of the New Testament read the Old Testament with this same conviction. They saw the words of the Bible speaking directly to their own situation. They read with humility and with prayer.

The first step along this way of holy reading is listening to the Bible. Choose a biblical text that is not too long. This commentary breaks Hebrews and James into smaller sections. The purpose is to hear God's voice in your current situation, not to cover material or prepare lessons. Get into a comfortable position and maintain silence before God for several minutes. This prepares the heart to listen. Read slowly. Savor each word. Perhaps read aloud. Listen for a particular phrase that speaks to you. Ask God, "What are you trying to tell me today?"

The next step is to meditate on that particular phrase. That meditation may include slowly repeating the phrase that seems to be for you today. As you think deeply on it, you might even memorize it. Committing biblical passages to memory allows us to hold them in our hearts all day long. If you keep a journal, you might write the passage there. Let those words sink deeply into your heart.

Then pray those words back to God in your heart. Those words may call up visual images, smells, sounds, and feelings. Pay attention to what God is giving you in those words. Then respond in faith to what those words say to your heart. What do they call you to be and to do? Our humble response might take the form of praise, thanksgiving, joy, confession, or even cries of pain.

The final step in this "holy reading" is contemplation of God. The words from God that we receive deeply in our hearts lead us to him. Through these words, we experience union with the all-powerful God of love. Again, one should not separate Bible reading from prayer. The words of God in Scripture transport us into the very presence of God where we joyfully rest in his love.

What keeps reading the Bible this way from becoming merely our own desires read back into Scripture? How do we know it is God's voice we hear and not our own?

Two things. One is prayer. We are asking God to open our hearts, minds, and lives to him. We ask to hear his voice, not ours and not the voice of the world around us.

The second thing that keeps this from being an exercise in self-deception is to study the Bible in community. By praying over

Scripture in a group, we hear God's word together. God speaks through the other members of our group. The wisdom he gives them keeps us from private, selfish, and unusual interpretations. They help us keep our own voices in check, as we desire to listen to God alone.

HOW TO USE THIS COMMENTARY

This commentary provides assistance in holy reading of the Bible. It gives structure to daily personal devotions, family meditation, small group Bible studies, and church classes.

DAILY DEVOTIONAL

Listening, meditation, prayer, contemplation. How does this commentary fit into this way of Bible study? Consider it as a conversation partner. We have taken a section of Scripture and then broken it down into four short daily readings. After listening, meditating, praying, and contemplating the passage for the day, use the questions suggested in the commentary to provoke deeper reflection. This provides a structure for a daily fifteen minute devotional four days a week. On the fifth day, read the entire passage, meditate, and then use the questions to reflect on the meaning of the whole. On day six, take our meditations on the passage as conversation with another who has prayed over the text.

If you want to begin daily Bible reading, but need guidance, this provides a Monday-Saturday experience that prepares the heart for worship and praise on Sunday. This structure also results in a communal reading of Scripture, instead of a private reading. Even if you use this commentary alone, you are not reading privately. God is at work in you and in the conversation you have with another (the author of the commentary) who has sought to hear God through this passage of the Bible.

FAMILY BIBLE STUDY

This commentary can also provide an arrangement for family Bible study. Many Christian parents want to lead their children in daily study, but don't know where to begin or how to structure their time. Using the six-day plan outlined above means the entire family can read, meditate, pray, and reflect on the shorter passages, using the questions provided. On day five, they can review the entire passage, and then on day six, read the meditations in the commentary to prompt reflection and discussion. God will bless our families beyond our imaginations through the prayerful study of his word.

WEEKLY GROUP STUDY

This commentary can also structure small group Bible study. Each member of the group should have meditated over the daily readings and questions for the five days preceding the group meeting, using the method outlined above. The day before the group meeting, each member should read and reflect on the meditations in the commentary on that passage. You then can meet once a week to hear God's word together. In that group meeting, the method of holy reading would look something like this:

Listening
1. Five minutes of silence.
2. Slow reading of the biblical passage for that week.

3. A minute of silent meditation on the passage.

4. Briefly share with the group the word or phrase that struck you.

Personal Message

5. A second reading of the same passage.

6. A minute of silence.

7. Where does this touch your life today?

8. Responses: I hear, I see, etc.

Life Response

9. Brief silence.

10. What does God want you to do today in light of this word?

Group Prayer

11. Have each member of the group pray aloud for the person on his or her left, asking God to bless the word he has given them.

The procedure suggested here can be used in churches or in neighborhood Bible studies. Church members would use the daily readings Monday-Friday in their daily devotionals. This commentary intentionally provides no readings on the sixth day, so that we can spend Saturdays as a time of rest, not rest from Bible study, but a time to let God's word quietly work its way deep into our hearts. Sunday during Bible school or in home meetings, the group would meet to experience the weekly readings together, using the group method described above. It might be that the sermon for each Sunday could be on the passage for that week.

Some churches have used this structure to great advantage. In the hallways of those church buildings, the talk is not of the local football team or the weather, but of the shared experience of the Word of God for that week.

And that is the purpose of our personal and communal study, to hear the voice of God, our loving Father who wants us to love him in return. He deeply desires a personal relationship with us. Father, Son, and Spirit make a home inside us (see John 14:16-17, 23). Our loving God speaks to his children! But we must listen for his voice. That listening is not a matter of gritting our teeth and trying harder to hear. Instead, it is part of our entire life with God. That is what Bible study is all about.

Through daily personal prayer and meditation on God's word and through a communal reading of Scripture, our most important conversation partner, the Holy Spirit, will do his mysterious and marvelous work. Among other things, the Spirit pours God's love into our hearts (Romans 5:5), bears witness to our spirits that we are God's children (Romans 8:16), intercedes for us with God (Romans 8:26), and enlightens us as to God's will (Ephesians 1:17).

So this is an invitation to personal daily Bible study, to praying the Scriptures, to sharing with fellow believers, to hear the voice of God. God will bless us, our families, our churches, and his world if we take the time to be still, listen, and do his word.

HEBREWS: KEEP YOUR EYES ON JESUS

THE SPIRITUALITY OF HEBREWS

Hebrews is a word of encouragement to tired Christians in danger of drifting away from the faith. This letter (or sermon) constantly points to Jesus as both divine and human. As God, he has the power to save us. As human, he saves with a gentle and sympathetic hand. The Spirit in Hebrews always leads us to Jesus our brother, High Priest, and example of trust in God.

THE SPIRIT SPEAKS

Hebrews often begins scripture quotations with the words, "As the Holy Spirit says." The Spirit thus is the ultimate source of scripture. God has not abandoned us to find truth and meaning on our own. He has spoken through his Son (Hebrews 1:2) and in the scriptures through his Spirit. The spirituality of Hebrews is first of all, a biblical spirituality.

THE SPIRIT OF GRACE

In Hebrews, the Spirit is intimately involved in our salvation. He points to Jesus, our High Priest. He confirms the word of eyewitnesses of Jesus through signs, wonders, miracles, and gifts (Hebrews 2:4). He is the Spirit of grace (Hebrews 10:29). Salvation means we share in this Spirit (Hebrews 6:4). Jesus offered himself for us through the eternal Spirit (Hebrews 9:14). The focus is on Jesus in Hebrews, but the work of Jesus is also the work of the Spirit. Spirituality in Hebrews is personal identification with Jesus through the shared experience of the Holy Spirit.

THE SPIRIT OF TRUSTING ENDURANCE

At the heart of Hebrews is a call to trusting endurance. God's people have always been called to leave a comfortable place and to trust God to lead them to a place they do not know. We can only have that trust through the work of the Spirit who confirms the love of God in Jesus. Spirituality in Hebrews means abandoning the city we know, suffering with Jesus outside the city, and looking for that lasting city that is to come. Tired, discouraged, disillusioned Christians desperately need to hear this encouraging word of trust.

MEDITATIONS

THE GREATEST

(Hebrews 1:1-2:4)

DAY ONE READING AND QUESTIONS:

¹In the past God spoke to our forefathers through the prophets at many times and in various ways, ²but in these last days he has spoken to us by his Son, whom he appointed heir of all things, and through whom he made the universe. ³The Son is the radiance of God's glory and the exact representation of his being, sustaining all things by his powerful word. After he had provided purification for sins, he sat down at the right hand of the Majesty in heaven. ⁴So he became as much superior to the angels as the name he has inherited is superior to theirs.

1. *List some ways God spoke in the Old Testament. Why do you think God spoke in so many different ways?*

2. *List seven things this passage says about the Son. Why does it describe him in such exalted ways?*

3. *Why is it important that God speaks to his people? Why is it important that the Son is God's last and best word to us?*

DAY TWO READING AND QUESTIONS

[5]For to which of the angels did God ever say,

    "You are my Son;

    today I have become your Father"?

Or again,

    "I will be his Father,

    and he will be my Son"?

[6]And again, when God brings his firstborn into the world, he

    says,

    "Let all God's angels worship him."

[7]In speaking of the angels he says,

    "He makes his angels winds,

    his servants flames of fire."

[8]But about the Son he says,

    "Your throne, O God, will last for ever and ever,

    and righteousness will be the scepter of your kingdom.

[9]You have loved righteousness and hated wickedness;

    therefore God, your God, has set you above your companions

    by anointing you with the oil of joy."

1. *Describe angels. Who are they? What do they do? Why do you think people are so interested in angels?*

2. *What are the contrasts here between the Son and the angels?*

3. *Why is it important that Jesus is greater than angels?*

Day Three Reading and Questions:

[10]He also says,

"In the beginning, O Lord, you laid the foundations
of the earth,
and the heavens are the work of your hands.
[11]They will perish, but you remain;
they will all wear out like a garment.
[12]You will roll them up like a robe;
like a garment they will be changed.
But you remain the same,
and your years will never end."
[13]To which of the angels did God ever say,
"Sit at my right hand
until I make your enemies
a footstool for your feet"?
[14]Are not all angels ministering spirits sent to serve those who will
inherit salvation?

1. *What is the role of the Son in creation? Why is this important?
How is it different from the role of angels?*

2. *What does it mean that the Son is at the right hand of the Father?
Why is that important?*

3. *How do angels serve us?*

Day Four Reading and Questions:

[1]We must pay more careful attention, therefore, to what we have
heard, so that we do not drift away. [2]For if the message spoken by

angels was binding, and every violation and disobedience received its just punishment, [3]how shall we escape if we ignore such a great salvation? This salvation, which was first announced by the Lord, was confirmed to us by those who heard him. [4]God also testified to it by signs, wonders and various miracles, and gifts of the Holy Spirit distributed according to his will.

1. *What was the message spoken by angels? What happened to those who disobeyed that message?*

2. *What makes our salvation so great?*

3. *What is the role of the Holy Spirit in salvation according to this passage?*

Day Five Reading and Questions:

Go back and read the entire passage.

1. *What is the point (the "therefore") of placing so much emphasis on the Son in this passage?*

2. *What are some ways we and others might ignore our great salvation? What might keep us from ignoring it?*

3. *Are we more likely suddenly to decide we are no longer Christians or more likely to drift away from what we have heard? What are some signs of drifting away?*

MEDITATION ON HEBREWS 1:1-2:4

What a great Savior! The Son of God, creator and sustainer of the universe. One who shares God's being and radiates his glory. The Son who purified us from sin by his death, who was raised from the dead, and now sits in the highest place of honor—the right hand of God.

He's even greater than the angels! Angels—powerful beings, bright as the sun, frightening in appearance, messengers of God. But angels are creatures just as we are. The Son is creator. Angels serve us. Every knee bows in service before the Son. What a great Savior!

What a great salvation! The Son completely purifies us from sin. We are free from sin, guilt, and shame once for all. The Son takes broken human creatures and exalts us to be with him at God's right hand.

What a great message! God has given us his last and best word, the Son of God, the word made flesh. God has confirmed his message with miracles, signs, and gifts through his Holy Spirit. No greater Savior. No greater salvation. No greater message.

So how can that message be so ho-hum to us? Jesus is the Son of God. We knew that. He is Creator, Sustainer, Redeemer. That's old hat to us. We take the great salvation for granted. We grow tired of the old, old story. We don't get excited by the message anymore.

We stand in danger. Of drifting. Of ignoring. Of neglecting. God loved us so much that he sent his Son. What more can he do? What more can he say? How much greater a salvation can there be?

"How shall we escape?" The words sound ominous. They sound as if the writer of Hebrews is trying to scare us into obedience. But it is right to scare others if the danger is real. It is. We must not drift, neglect, and ignore the greatest gift of all. The greatest Savior. The greatest salvation. The greatest message.

"Father, this day bring your Son before our eyes. May we know the indescribable depth of your love. May we pay close attention and not drift or ignore."

ONE OF US

(Hebrews 2:5-18)

Day One Reading and Questions:

⁵It is not to angels that he has subjected the world to come, about which we are speaking. ⁶But there is a place where someone has testified:
"What is man that you are mindful of him,
    the son of man that you care for him?
⁷You made him a little lower than the angels;
    you crowned him with glory and honor
        ⁸and put everything under his feet."
In putting everything under him, God left nothing that is not subject to him. Yet at present we do not see everything subject to him.

1. Who is the "him" in this passage, human beings or Jesus? Could it be both? How?

2. How can everything be subject to him, yet we do not see everything subject to him at present? Does Jesus rule our world or not?

3. Verse seven can be translated, "you made him for a little while lower than the angels..." How does this change the meaning of the passage?

DAY TWO READING AND QUESTIONS:

[9] But we see Jesus, who was made a little lower than the angels, now crowned with glory and honor because he suffered death, so that by the grace of God he might taste death for everyone.

[10]In bringing many sons to glory, it was fitting that God, for whom and through whom everything exists, should make the author of their salvation perfect through suffering. [11]Both the one who makes men holy and those who are made holy are of the same family. So Jesus is not ashamed to call them brothers. [12]He says,

"I will declare your name to my brothers;
   in the presence of the congregation I will sing your praises."[13]And again,
   "I will put my trust in him." And again he says,
   "Here am I, and the children God has given me."

1. *Why is Jesus now crowned with glory and honor? What is the connection between suffering and glory?*

2. *How is Jesus made perfect? Was he not perfect from all eternity? What does perfecting mean here?*

3. *What two things does Jesus call us here? How does that make you feel?*

DAY THREE READING AND QUESTIONS:

[14]Since the children have flesh and blood, he too shared in their humanity so that by his death he might destroy him who holds the power of death—that is, the devil— [15]and free those who all their lives were held in slavery by their fear of death.

1. Did Jesus have flesh and blood just like we do? If so, what did he feel? What challenges did he face?

2. Do you fear death? Why? Is it normal to fear death? Did Jesus fear death?

3. How did Jesus overcome the power of death?

DAY FOUR READING AND QUESTIONS:

[16]For surely it is not angels he helps, but Abraham's descendants. [17]For this reason he had to be made like his brothers in every way, in order that he might become a merciful and faithful high priest in service to God, and that he might make atonement for the sins of the people. [18]Because he himself suffered when he was tempted, he is able to help those who are being tempted.

1. Is Jesus like us in every way? Is that hard to believe? Why?

2. This is the first time the idea of high priest occurs in Hebrews. What is a high priest? What does he do? How is Jesus our high priest?

3. Why does temptation make us suffer? Did Jesus suffer more or less from temptation than we do? Why?

DAY FIVE READING AND QUESTIONS:

Go back and read the entire passage.

1. Do we often call Jesus our brother? Why or why not?

2. Could Jesus have sinned when he was tempted? What would have happened if he had? How real were his temptations? Why is it important to us that they were real?

3. What are the ways Jesus helps us in this passage?

MEDITATION ON HEBREWS 2:5-18

Jesus is the very image of God.
I can believe that.
Jesus is greater than the angels.
Of course, that's true.
Jesus is human like me. He calls me his brother. He's not ashamed to be like me.
I find that hard to believe.

My guess is that I am not alone. While some may find it hard to buy the divinity of Jesus, that he is fully God, many Christians I know do not truly believe he was just like us. Oh yes, he had a body. Yes he was hungry and thirsty. But just like me? Tempted to be selfish, petty, grouchy, and egotistical? Tired? Bored? Sexual? Did he really experience all it means to be human?

Yes. He had to be like his brothers and sisters in every way. *Every* way.

But Jesus did not sin. So he could not be human like us. "To err is human" (which is not a Bible verse).

No, he did not sin, but he could have. To say otherwise would be to deny this passage and the temptation stories in the Gospels. If Jesus could not sin, then he was not truly tempted. But he was tempted, part of him wanted to do the wrong thing because the wrong thing looked so good (isn't that what we mean by temptation?). But it is not wrong to be tempted. It's merely human. Temptation is not sin.

Jesus suffered in temptation, suffered more than we do. How? Well, at times when I am tempted, I do not suffer long because I give in! Jesus never gave in. He faced the full struggle with temptation. Because he did, he can help us when we are tempted.

How great is Jesus? Son of God. Creator. Lord of the angels. How great is Jesus? So great that he became one of us to be our High Priest, to forgive our sins, and to be our brother.

He is so great that he is not ashamed of us.

"Brother Jesus, may we feel your loving presence with us this day, particularly in time of trial. As you are not ashamed of us, may we never be ashamed of you."

TRUST IN REST

(Hebrews 3:1-4:13)

Day One Reading and Questions

[1]Therefore, holy brothers, who share in the heavenly calling, fix your thoughts on Jesus, the apostle and high priest whom we confess. [2]He was faithful to the one who appointed him, just as Moses was faithful in all God's house. [3]Jesus has been found worthy of greater honor than Moses, just as the builder of a house has greater honor than the house itself. [4]For every house is built by someone, but God is the builder of everything. [5]Moses was faithful as a servant in all God's house, testifying to what would be said in the future. [6]But Christ is faithful as a son over God's house. And we are his house, if we hold on to our courage and the hope of which we boast.

1. *What does it mean to fix our thoughts on Jesus? Is this more than thinking about him? What specifically should we "fix" on concerning Jesus?*

2. *How is Jesus like Moses? How is he different?*

3. *How are we God's house?*

Day Two Reading and Questions:

[7]So, as the Holy Spirit says:

"Today, if you hear his voice,
    [8]do not harden your hearts
    as you did in the rebellion,
    during the time of testing in the desert,
[9]where your fathers tested and tried me
    and for forty years saw what I did.
[10]That is why I was angry with that generation,
    and I said, 'Their hearts are always going astray,
    and they have not known my ways.'
[11]So I declared on oath in my anger,
    'They shall never enter my rest.' ' "

[12]See to it, brothers, that none of you has a sinful, unbelieving heart that turns away from the living God. [13]But encourage one another daily, as long as it is called Today, so that none of you may be hardened by sin's deceitfulness. [14]We have come to share in Christ if we hold firmly till the end the confidence we had at first. [15]As has just been said:

"Today, if you hear his voice,
    do not harden your hearts
    as you did in the rebellion."

1. Why did God not allow the generation in the wilderness to enter his rest? What Bible story does this refer to?

2. What will keep us from having sinful, unbelieving hearts?

3. List some ways we can encourage one another daily toward trusting God.

DAY THREE READING AND QUESTIONS:

[16]Who were they who heard and rebelled? Were they not all those Moses led out of Egypt? [17]And with whom was he angry for forty years? Was it not with those who sinned, whose bodies fell in the desert? [18]And to whom did God swear that they would never enter his rest if not to those who disobeyed? [19]So we see that they were not able to enter, because of their unbelief.

[1]Therefore, since the promise of entering his rest still stands, let us be careful that none of you be found to have fallen short of it. [2]For we also have had the gospel preached to us, just as they did; but the message they heard was of no value to them, because those who heard did not combine it with faith. [3]Now we who have believed enter that rest, just as God has said,

"So I declared on oath in my anger,

'They shall never enter my rest.'

"And yet his work has been finished since the creation of the world. [4]For somewhere he has spoken about the seventh day in these words: "And on the seventh day God rested from all his work." [5]And again in the passage above he says, "They shall never enter my rest."

1. *In what sense does the promise of rest remain? What is the rest we are promised by God?*

2. *How could we fall short of that rest? Why does this warning occur in a book meant to encourage us? Can warnings help us?*

3. *Describe the anger of God. How is it different from human anger?*

Day Four Reading and Questions:

[6]It still remains that some will enter that rest, and those who formerly had the gospel preached to them did not go in, because of their disobedience. [7]Therefore God again set a certain day, calling it Today, when a long time later he spoke through David, as was said before:

"Today, if you hear his voice,
do not harden your hearts."

[8]For if Joshua had given them rest, God would not have spoken later about another day. [9]There remains, then, a Sabbath-rest for the people of God; [10]for anyone who enters God's rest also rests from his own work, just as God did from his. [11]Let us, therefore, make every effort to enter that rest, so that no one will fall by following their example of disobedience.

[12]For the word of God is living and active. Sharper than any double-edged sword, it penetrates even to dividing soul and spirit, joints and marrow; it judges the thoughts and attitudes of the heart. [13]Nothing in all creation is hidden from God's sight. Everything is uncovered and laid bare before the eyes of him to whom we must give account.

1. *What is the relationship between unbelief and disobedience? How did Israel's unbelief lead to disobedience?*

2. *We are told to make every effort to enter God's rest. Is this works righteousness and earning salvation? How does our effort relate to God's grace?*

3. *What is the point of the sword illustration? Whose sword is it? What does it do? How does this sword illustration relate to the rest God promised?*

Day Five Reading and Questions:

Go back and read the entire passage.

1. *Do you need more rest? What kind of rest does Jesus promise us in this passage?*

2. *Why do we fail to receive the gift of rest Jesus promised?*

3. *Is it urgent to enter God's rest? When should we listen to God's voice?*

MEDITATION ON HEBREWS 3:1-4:13

I wake up in the morning thinking, "I can't wait to get some rest. Wonder if I can work in a nap today."

Perhaps it's my age creeping up on me, but I don't think I'm alone. The college students I teach drag themselves to class, needing sleep. Overworked mothers get no rest. No matter what business they are in, my friends all long for the day off, the weekend, and the vacation.

We live in an age that needs some rest.

God promises rest. Not simply a day off or an extended vacation, but a deep, daily, satisfying rest. God invites us into his very life, the rest he has enjoyed since creation. That invitation is urgent ("Today") and personal.

But for most of us, serving God doesn't look like rest, it looks like more work! Church meetings, small groups, and committee work all pile up as more things to do on an already too busy schedule.

So what is this rest God promises? How do we enter it? The same way Jesus did. The same way Moses did. By being faithful. Trusting.

Listening. With soft, not hard hearts. We enter that rest by trusting the promises of God today.

That rest is not something way out there in our future—when we die by and by—it is a reality every moment of each day. By allowing God's word to cut deeply into our hearts, we open ourselves to that daily work that is rest. As Jesus himself said, "Come to me, all you who are weary and burdened, and I will give you rest. Take my yoke upon you and learn from me, for I am gentle and humble in heart, and you will find rest for your souls. For my yoke is easy and my burden is light" (Matthew 11:28-30).

The secret of the easy yoke is trust. If, like Jesus, we are faithful in God's house, then each moment spent with God is a place of deep, satisfying rest.

"Father, we are so tired because we run our own lives. May we trust our little lives with you, knowing that you alone bring rest."

ON TO MATURITY

(Hebrews 4:14-6:3)

DAY ONE READING AND QUESTIONS:

[14]Therefore, since we have a great high priest who has gone through the heavens, Jesus the Son of God, let us hold firmly to the faith we profess. [15]For we do not have a high priest who is unable to sympathize with our weaknesses, but we have one who has been tempted in every way, just as we are—yet was without sin. [16]Let us then approach the throne of grace with confidence, so that we may receive mercy and find grace to help us in our time of need.

[1]Every high priest is selected from among men and is appointed to represent them in matters related to God, to offer gifts and sacrifices for sins. [2]He is able to deal gently with those who are ignorant and are going astray, since he himself is subject to weakness. [3]This is why he has to offer sacrifices for his own sins, as well as for the sins of the people.

1. What does a high priest do?

2. What is there about Jesus as a high priest that allows us to approach God with confidence?

3. Do we need our high priest to deal gently with us? Do we deal gently with others?

DAY TWO READING AND QUESTIONS:

[4]No one takes this honor upon himself; he must be called by God, just as Aaron was. [5]So Christ also did not take upon himself the glory of becoming a high priest. But God said to him,

"You are my Son;

today I have become your Father."

[6]And he says in another place,

"You are a priest forever,

in the order of Melchizedek."

[7]During the days of Jesus' life on earth, he offered up prayers and petitions with loud cries and tears to the one who could save him from death, and he was heard because of his reverent submission. [8]Although he was a son, he learned obedience from what he suffered [9]and, once made perfect, he became the source of eternal salvation for all who obey him [10]and was designated by God to be high priest in the order of Melchizedek.

1. How did God call Jesus to be high priest?

2. When did Jesus offer loud cries and tears to God? How was he heard? Did God save him from death?

3. How was Jesus "made perfect"? Wasn't he already perfect?

DAY THREE READING AND QUESTIONS:

[11]We have much to say about this, but it is hard to explain because you are slow to learn. [12]In fact, though by this time you ought to be teachers, you need someone to teach you the elementary truths of God's word all over again. You need milk, not solid food! [13]Anyone who lives on milk, being still an infant, is not acquainted with the teaching about righteousness. [14]But solid food is for the mature, who by constant use have trained themselves to distinguish good from evil.

> *1. What makes these readers slow to learn? Are they not smart enough to understand?*

> *2. What is the point of the milk and meat illustration? How do these readers need to grow up?*

> *3. Why would the writer of Hebrews criticize his readers this way? Isn't this negative? Wouldn't this discourage them from reading?*

DAY FOUR READING AND QUESTIONS:

[1]Therefore let us leave the elementary teachings about Christ and go on to maturity, not laying again the foundation of repentance from acts that lead to death, and of faith in God, [2]instruction about baptisms, the laying on of hands, the resurrection of the dead, and eternal judgment. [3]And God permitting, we will do so.

> *1. What does it mean to leave the elementary teachings of Christ? Does that mean we no longer believe these things?*

2. What six things are listed here as elementary teachings?

3. If you were listing the elementary teachings of Christianity, would this be your list? What might you leave out? What would you add?

Day Five Reading and Questions:

Go back and read the entire passage.

1. What is the relationship between Jesus as our High Priest and becoming mature?

2. Why are many Christians not as mature as they should be? What should be done to prevent this?

3. What does maturity have to do with distinguishing good from evil? What kind of maturity is spoken of here?

MEDITATION ON HEBREWS 4:14-6:3

High Priest. The concept seems so strange. Someone to stand between God and us. Why do we need that? Can't we go to God on our own?

Yes and no. God is a loving Father who always waits for us to come to him. He is the Father of the lost boy who returns. He runs to meet us with shoes, and robe, and ring. He throws a party to celebrate our return (Luke 15).

So why do we need a High Priest? Because we are ashamed and embarrassed to come to God. Have you ever done something stupid and offended your boss. You want to go to him and make amends, but you're not sure if you should or how you should. You need someone to smooth the way.

We are more than embarrassed before God. We do not have a leg to stand on before him. There are a million and one reasons why he should send us all to hell and only one reason why he should forgive.

But what a reason! Jesus, the Son of God, offering himself as sacrifice for us. Jesus our High Priest, called by God but sharing in our cries and tears.

Why is it we may not appreciate this great gift of a High Priest? Maybe because we are spiritually immature. We should know right from wrong by now. We should be teachers, letting others know of this marvelous gift. Instead, we are slow to learn the depth of God's love for us.

"Loving Father, open the eyes of our hearts to see Jesus our great High Priest. May we feel the depth of your love and teach others your grace."

HOLD ON TO HOPE

(Hebrews 6:4-20)

Day One Reading and Questions:

[4]It is impossible for those who have once been enlightened, who have tasted the heavenly gift, who have shared in the Holy Spirit, [5]who have tasted the goodness of the word of God and the powers of the coming age, [6]if they fall away, to be brought back to repentance, because to their loss they are crucifying the Son of God all over again and subjecting him to public disgrace.

1. *Should we worry that we have fallen away so much from God that we cannot return?*

2. *Is the writer of Hebrews trying to scare us? Is it good to scare people into following God?*

3. *What does it mean to crucify Christ afresh? Are there many ways to do this?*

Day Two Reading and Questions:

[7]Land that drinks in the rain often falling on it and that produces a crop useful to those for whom it is farmed receives the blessing of God. [8]But land that produces thorns and thistles is worthless and is in danger of being cursed. In the end it will be burned.

[9]Even though we speak like this, dear friends, we are confident of better things in your case—things that accompany salvation. [10]God is not unjust; he will not forget your work and the love you have shown him as you have helped his people and continue to help them. [11]We want each of you to show this same diligence to the very end, in order to make your hope sure. [12]We do not want you to become lazy, but to imitate those who through faith and patience inherit what has been promised.

1. *What is the point of the land illustration? Who is the land that drinks in the rain?*

2. *Is it comforting to know God will not forget our works of love? Do we sometimes feel others forget them? Give examples from your own life.*

3. *What is diligence? Does showing diligence mean we are earning our salvation through good works? What does it mean? Why is it encouraged here?*

Day Three Reading and Questions:

[13]When God made his promise to Abraham, since there was no one greater for him to swear by, he swore by himself, [14]saying, "I will surely bless you and give you many descendants." [15]And so after waiting patiently, Abraham received what was promised. [16]Men swear by someone greater than themselves, and the oath

confirms what is said and puts an end to all argument. [17]Because God wanted to make the unchanging nature of his purpose very clear to the heirs of what was promised, he confirmed it with an oath.

1. *What is the purpose of swearing? Is it strange that God himself would swear?*

2. *How long did Abraham have to wait for God's promises to come true? How long must we wait for his promises to come true?*

3. *Why might we lose faith in the unchanging nature of God's purpose? How does God strengthen our patient faith?*

Day Four Reading and Questions:

[18]God did this so that, by two unchangeable things in which it is impossible for God to lie, we who have fled to take hold of the hope offered to us may be greatly encouraged. [19]We have this hope as an anchor for the soul, firm and secure. It enters the inner sanctuary behind the curtain, [20]where Jesus, who went before us, has entered on our behalf. He has become a high priest forever, in the order of Melchizedek.

1. *What are the "two unchangeable things in which it is impossible for God to lie"?*

2. *How is our hope like an anchor?*

3. *How does hope enter the inner sanctuary of God? In the Old Testament, who was allowed to enter that Most Holy Place? What does that say about our standing before God?*

DAY FIVE READING AND QUESTIONS:

Go back and read the entire passage.

1. *How do we know we can trust God? Why is it sometimes hard to trust?*

2. *If we lose our faith and hope in God, might we drift so far away from him that we cannot return? If so, what can keep us from this drifting?*

3. *List some aspects of our world that slowly work to erode our faith and hope in God. How can we overcome this loss?*

MEDITATION ON HEBREWS 6:4-20

Hope is a fragile thing.

Many of us have placed our hope in people we trust—husbands, wives, elected officials, financial advisors, church leaders, and friends—only to have those hopes crushed. Hope can disappear in a moment, through disappointment, betrayal, and disillusionment.

"Disillusionment." An interesting word. Our illusions of hope vanish, leaving us with a deep cynicism, cursing ourselves for being taken in by those we trusted who made empty promises.

We can even lose our hope in God. No, we don't want to admit it, not to our friends, our families, or even ourselves. We continue to go through the motions of church, prayer, and Bible reading, but deep down we don't think anything will change.

We are in danger of losing faith. Abandoning hope. Falling away.

What can we do?

There's nothing left to do but to trust God.

That answer seems too churchy and religious. It might even seem impossible. If we are losing our faith, how can we trust more?

By changing our focus. By looking away from our pain and disappointment to set our sight on the God who promises. He is a God who keeps his word, but if we ever doubt that, he is also the God who swears to us. He takes an oath to convince us he is honest in his promises.

Faith must be fed. Hope must be nurtured. Love must be shown to others in quiet acts of service. We can so abandon hope that return to God is impossible. But God does all he can to keep hope alive. He is the God who blesses. He sends the rain on our parched lives. He enlightens us, feeds us, and shares his very life with us through his Holy Spirit. He sent his Son as our High Priest. When we begin to feel that hope is an illusion, we must look at Jesus. Others will fail us. He alone is our hope and he will not disappoint. Our trust in him is no illusion.

"Father, increase our trust in you through Jesus. Give us that sure hope that never disappoints. May we live hopeful lives this day."

OUR GREAT PRIEST

(Hebrews 7:1-8:5)

Day One Reading and Questions:

¹This Melchizedek was king of Salem and priest of God Most High. He met Abraham returning from the defeat of the kings and blessed him, ²and Abraham gave him a tenth of everything. First, his name means "king of righteousness"; then also, "king of Salem" means "king of peace." ³Without father or mother, without genealogy, without beginning of days or end of life, like the Son of God he remains a priest forever.

⁴Just think how great he was: Even the patriarch Abraham gave him a tenth of the plunder! ⁵Now the law requires the descendants of Levi who become priests to collect a tenth from the people—that is, their brothers—even though their brothers are descended from Abraham. ⁶This man, however, did not trace his descent from Levi, yet he collected a tenth from Abraham and blessed him who had the promises. ⁷And without doubt the lesser person is blessed by the greater. ⁸In the one case, the tenth is collected by men who die; but in the other case, by him who is declared to be living. ⁹One might even say that Levi, who collects the tenth, paid the tenth through Abraham, ¹⁰because when Melchizedek met Abraham, Levi was still in the body of his ancestor.

1. Read the Melchizedek story in Genesis 14:18-20. Is Melchizedek a major character in the Old Testament? Why does Hebrews emphasize him so much?

2. Did Melchizedek literally have no mother or father? If he did, what does "without father or mother, without genealogy, without beginning of days or end of life" mean?

3. How does this passage make Melchizedek's priesthood greater than the Levitical priesthood?

Day Two Reading and Questions:

[11]If perfection could have been attained through the Levitical priesthood (for on the basis of it the law was given to the people), why was there still need for another priest to come—one in the order of Melchizedek, not in the order of Aaron? [12]For when there is a change of the priesthood, there must also be a change of the law. [13]He of whom these things are said belonged to a different tribe, and no one from that tribe has ever served at the altar. [14]For it is clear that our Lord descended from Judah, and in regard to that tribe Moses said nothing about priests. [15]And what we have said is even more clear if another priest like Melchizedek appears, [16]one who has become a priest not on the basis of a regulation as to his ancestry but on the basis of the power of an indestructible life. [17]For it is declared:

"You are a priest forever,
      in the order of Melchizedek."
[18]The former regulation is set aside because it was weak and useless [19](for the law made nothing perfect), and a better hope is introduced, by which we draw near to God.

1. What does it mean that there is a change of the law? In Christ, are we under a law? If so, how is it different from the old law?

2. Why is the former law or regulation weak and useless? Does this mean that God gave Israel a bad law?

3. Why is our hope a better hope than what they had under the old law?

Day Three Reading and Questions:

[20]And it was not without an oath! Others became priests without any oath, [21]but he became a priest with an oath when God said to him:
"The Lord has sworn
> and will not change his mind:
> 'You are a priest forever.'"
[22]Because of this oath, Jesus has become the guarantee of a better covenant.

[23]Now there have been many of those priests, since death prevented them from continuing in office; [24]but because Jesus lives forever, he has a permanent priesthood. [25]Therefore he is able to save completely those who come to God through him, because he always lives to intercede for them.

[26]Such a high priest meets our need—one who is holy, blameless, pure, set apart from sinners, exalted above the heavens. [27]Unlike the other high priests, he does not need to offer sacrifices day after day, first for his own sins, and then for the sins of the people. He sacrificed for their sins once for all when he offered himself. [28]For the law appoints as high priests men who are weak; but the oath, which came after the law, appointed the Son, who has been made perfect forever.

1. *Name three ways that Jesus has a better priesthood than the Levitical priests, according to this passage.*

2. *How does Jesus make intercession for us? Why do we need this so much?*

3. *What does it mean that Jesus is "set apart from sinners"? Don't we need Jesus to be near us as sinners?*

Day Four Reading and Questions:

[1]The point of what we are saying is this: We do have such a high priest, who sat down at the right hand of the throne of the Majesty in heaven, [2]and who serves in the sanctuary, the true tabernacle set up by the Lord, not by man.

[3]Every high priest is appointed to offer both gifts and sacrifices, and so it was necessary for this one also to have something to offer. [4]If he were on earth, he would not be a priest, for there are already men who offer the gifts prescribed by the law. [5]They serve at a sanctuary that is a copy and shadow of what is in heaven. This is why Moses was warned when he was about to build the tabernacle: "See to it that you make everything according to the pattern shown you on the mountain."

1. *Why is it significant that Jesus serves in the true tabernacle, not the copy?*

2. *What sacrifice does Jesus have to offer?*

3. *Why is it important that Jesus is at the right hand of God and not on the earth?*

DAY FIVE READING AND QUESTIONS:

Go back and read the entire passage.

1. Why does Hebrews use such obscure ideas like Melchizedek, priest-hood, and tabernacle to make his point? Do you have trouble identifying with these words?

2. How does this section fit with the one before it (Hebrews 6:4-20)? What is the major theme of both sections?

3. What does a high priest do? Why do we need one? How is Jesus our High Priest?

MEDITATION ON HEBREWS 7:1-8:5

Having a priest is a strange idea to me. "Priest" smacks of ritual, religion, and magic. Having to go through a priest to get to God doesn't sound very democratic. I've always been taught that we don't need a priest to go to God for us. We can approach God for ourselves.

What an arrogant notion, that we can approach God for ourselves! Do we really think we can stand before the Almighty, the Holy One, and be proud of who we are? Surely we know better. We are limited. Human. Finite. Broken. Sinful. Confused.

Who can stand before God?

We can. But not on our own. We need a priest who stands there for us and with us. We need one who takes care of our sins, heals our brokenness, and saves us completely. We need one to intercede. We need one who one who is holy, blameless, pure, set apart from sinners, exalted above the heavens.

The great and good news is that we have such a priest. All that we read here of oaths, tabernacles, patterns, and Melchizedek is to impress upon us the great gift God has given us in Jesus. He is our powerful High Priest, who sits at God's right hand to put in a good word for us. We can stand boldly before our God not because of what we are or what we have done, but because of what Jesus is and what he has done.

This is our better hope, a hope not in ourselves, but in our Savior.

"Lord Jesus, we thank and praise you as our great High Priest. May we rely not on ourselves, but on you."

REAL SALVATION

(Hebrews 8:6-9:28)

Day One Reading and Questions:

⁶But the ministry Jesus has received is as superior to theirs as the covenant of which he is mediator is superior to the old one, and it is founded on better promises.

⁷For if there had been nothing wrong with that first covenant, no place would have been sought for another. ⁸But God found fault with the people and said:

"The time is coming, declares the Lord,

when I will make a new covenant

with the house of Israel

and with the house of Judah.

⁹It will not be like the covenant

I made with their forefathers

when I took them by the hand

to lead them out of Egypt,

because they did not remain faithful to my covenant,

and I turned away from them, declares the Lord.

¹⁰This is the covenant I will make with the house of Israel

after that time, declares the Lord.

I will put my laws in their minds

and write them on their hearts.
I will be their God,
and they will be my people.
[11]No longer will a man teach his neighbor,
or a man his brother, saying, 'Know the Lord,'
because they will all know me,
from the least of them to the greatest.
[12]For I will forgive their wickedness
and will remember their sins no more."

[13]By calling this covenant "new," he has made the first one obsolete; and what is obsolete and aging will soon disappear.

1. *What exactly is a covenant? How is a covenant different from similar ideas like contact, deal, or agreement?*

2. *What makes this new covenant better than the old one?*

3. *What will God do in this new covenant?*

Day Two Reading and Questions:

[1]Now the first covenant had regulations for worship and also an earthly sanctuary. [2]A tabernacle was set up. In its first room were the lampstand, the table and the consecrated bread; this was called the Holy Place. [3]Behind the second curtain was a room called the Most Holy Place, [4]which had the golden altar of incense and the gold-covered ark of the covenant. This ark contained the gold jar of manna, Aaron's staff that had budded, and the stone tablets of the covenant. [5]Above the ark were the cherubim of the Glory, overshadowing the atonement cover. But we cannot discuss these things in detail now.

53

[6]When everything had been arranged like this, the priests entered regularly into the outer room to carry on their ministry. [7]But only the high priest entered the inner room, and that only once a year, and never without blood, which he offered for himself and for the sins the people had committed in ignorance. [8]The Holy Spirit was showing by this that the way into the Most Holy Place had not yet been disclosed as long as the first tabernacle was still standing. [9]This is an illustration for the present time, indicating that the gifts and sacrifices being offered were not able to clear the conscience of the worshiper. [10]They are only a matter of food and drink and various ceremonial washings—external regulations applying until the time of the new order.

1. *What is the point of describing all the furniture of the tabernacle? Is this more than Bible trivia?*

2. *How was access to the Most Holy Place (the "inner room") limited under the old covenant? How is this different under the new covenant?*

3. *Why were the gifts and sacrifices under the old covenant unable to cleanse the consciences of the worshipper? If they did not forgive sin, why did the people make those sacrifices?*

DAY THREE READING AND QUESTIONS:

[11]When Christ came as high priest of the good things that are already here, he went through the greater and more perfect tabernacle that is not man-made, that is to say, not a part of this creation. [12]He did not enter by means of the blood of goats and calves; but he entered the Most Holy Place once for all by his own blood, having obtained eternal redemption. [13]The blood of goats and bulls and the

ashes of a heifer sprinkled on those who are ceremonially unclean sanctify them so that they are outwardly clean. [14]How much more, then, will the blood of Christ, who through the eternal Spirit offered himself unblemished to God, cleanse our consciences from acts that lead to death, so that we may serve the living God!

[15]For this reason Christ is the mediator of a new covenant, that those who are called may receive the promised eternal inheritance—now that he has died as a ransom to set them free from the sins committed under the first covenant.

[16]In the case of a will, it is necessary to prove the death of the one who made it, [17]because a will is in force only when somebody has died; it never takes effect while the one who made it is living. [18]This is why even the first covenant was not put into effect without blood. [19]When Moses had proclaimed every commandment of the law to all the people, he took the blood of calves, together with water, scarlet wool and branches of hyssop, and sprinkled the scroll and all the people. [20]He said, "This is the blood of the covenant, which God has commanded you to keep." [21]In the same way, he sprinkled with the blood both the tabernacle and everything used in its ceremonies. [22]In fact, the law requires that nearly everything be cleansed with blood, and without the shedding of blood there is no forgiveness.

1. *What does the blood of Christ do for us?*

2. *How is our redemption an eternal redemption?*

3. *The word translated "will" here could also be translated "covenant." How is the covenant of Jesus his Last Will and Testament?*

Day Four Reading and Questions:

[23]It was necessary, then, for the copies of the heavenly things to be purified with these sacrifices, but the heavenly things themselves with better sacrifices than these. [24]For Christ did not enter a man-made sanctuary that was only a copy of the true one; he entered heaven itself, now to appear for us in God's presence. [25]Nor did he enter heaven to offer himself again and again, the way the high priest enters the Most Holy Place every year with blood that is not his own. [26]Then Christ would have had to suffer many times since the creation of the world. But now he has appeared once for all at the end of the ages to do away with sin by the sacrifice of himself. [27]Just as man is destined to die once, and after that to face judgment, [28]so Christ was sacrificed once to take away the sins of many people; and he will appear a second time, not to bear sin, but to bring salvation to those who are waiting for him.

1. *Why is it significant that Jesus offered himself once?*

2. *In what sense will the second coming of Christ bring salvation? Are we not already saved?*

3. *Why do you think this passage mentions that we are destined to die? Is this an encouraging message?*

Day Five Reading and Questions:

Go back and read the entire passage.

1. *Why is blood so important in this passage? Why is biblical religion so bloody? What place does such violent language have in a peaceful religion like Christianity?*

2. What is the significance of "once" or "once for all" in this passage?

3. What is the significance of "copy" in this passage? What is more real or genuine, an original or a copy?

MEDITATION ON HEBREWS 8:6-9:28

The genuine article is always more valuable than a copy. Whether paintings, baseball cards, or famous signatures, we want to know if what we have is real or a mere reproduction.

It's the same way with salvation. It's not as if God did not save his people in the Old Testament. He did. He led them out of Egypt, delivered them from their enemies, and gave them a system of sacrifices to forgive their sins. However, as wonderful as his covenant love was to them, it pales in comparison to his grace in Christ. Indeed, in light of what Jesus has done for us, their covenant was merely a copy, a shadow, or a reprint.

That's why the tabernacle furniture is important. Not as Bible trivia, but as a reminder that Christ is our High Priest in the true, heavenly tabernacle. His sacrifice (his own blood) is the real one. All the blood of bulls, sheep, and goats are mere imitations of that great sacrifice. Those sacrifices were offered daily. His is once for all. It is the genuine article that cleanses us completely.

This view of the real and the copy turns our usual way of thinking upside down. Most folks think the physical is real, but the spiritual is shadowy and unsubstantial. The Bible thinks the opposite. Yes the physical is real, but the spiritual is more real—more certain, more permanent, and more final.

Therefore we can put our complete trust in the salvation Jesus brings. It is real. It is genuine. God himself, by his oath and promise authenticates that salvation. Not only can we trust it, but we wait for it. Waiting for the time when Jesus returns. Waiting for the real thing.

"Our Savior, give us faith to believe you are real. May we trust your salvation until that day when you return and we see you face to face."

DRAW NEAR TO GOD

(Hebrews 10:1-31)

Day One Reading and Questions:

¹The law is only a shadow of the good things that are coming—not the realities themselves. For this reason it can never, by the same sacrifices repeated endlessly year after year, make perfect those who draw near to worship. ²If it could, would they not have stopped being offered? For the worshipers would have been cleansed once for all, and would no longer have felt guilty for their sins. ³But those sacrifices are an annual reminder of sins, ⁴because it is impossible for the blood of bulls and goats to take away sins.

⁵Therefore, when Christ came into the world, he said:

"Sacrifice and offering you did not desire,

but a body you prepared for me;

⁶with burnt offerings and sin offerings

you were not pleased.

⁷Then I said, 'Here I am—it is written about me in the scroll—

I have come to do your will, O God.' "

⁸First he said, "Sacrifices and offerings, burnt offerings and sin offerings you did not desire, nor were you pleased with them" (although the law required them to be made). ⁹Then he said, "Here I am, I have come to do your will." He sets aside the first to establish the

second. [10]And by that will, we have been made holy through the sacrifice of the body of Jesus Christ once for all.

1. If animal blood cannot take away sin, why did God command such sacrifices?

2. Jesus came to do God's will. What does this have to do with sacrifices?

3. If we have been made holy once for all through the sacrifice of Jesus, do we continue to feel guilty about our sins? Should we?

Day Two Reading and Questions:

[11]Day after day every priest stands and performs his religious duties; again and again he offers the same sacrifices, which can never take away sins. [12]But when this priest had offered for all time one sacrifice for sins, he sat down at the right hand of God. [13]Since that time he waits for his enemies to be made his footstool, [14]because by one sacrifice he has made perfect forever those who are being made holy.

[15]The Holy Spirit also testifies to us about this. First he says:
[16]"This is the covenant I will make with them
    after that time, says the Lord.
    I will put my laws in their hearts,
    and I will write them on their minds."
[17]Then he adds:
    "Their sins and lawless acts
    I will remember no more."
[18]And where these have been forgiven, there is no longer any sacrifice for sin.

1. *If the sacrifices offered at the temple can never take away sins, why did the priests offer them?*

2. *How does the sacrifice of Jesus make us perfect forever?*

3. *Why do we no longer need a sacrifice for sin?*

DAY THREE READING AND QUESTIONS:

[19]Therefore, brothers, since we have confidence to enter the Most Holy Place by the blood of Jesus, [20]by a new and living way opened for us through the curtain, that is, his body, [21]and since we have a great priest over the house of God, [22]let us draw near to God with a sincere heart in full assurance of faith, having our hearts sprinkled to cleanse us from a guilty conscience and having our bodies washed with pure water.

1. *Do you feel confident before God? What gives us confidence to enter God's presence?*

2. *What does it mean to have our hearts sprinkled? How does this change our lives?*

3. *Does having our bodies washed refer to baptism? If so, what happens in baptism?*

DAY FOUR READING AND QUESTIONS:

[23]Let us hold unswervingly to the hope we profess, for he who promised is faithful. [24]And let us consider how we may spur one another on toward love and good deeds. [25]Let us not give up meeting

together, as some are in the habit of doing, but let us encourage one another—and all the more as you see the Day approaching.

[26]If we deliberately keep on sinning after we have received the knowledge of the truth, no sacrifice for sins is left, [27]but only a fearful expectation of judgment and of raging fire that will consume the enemies of God. [28]Anyone who rejected the law of Moses died without mercy on the testimony of two or three witnesses. [29]How much more severely do you think a man deserves to be punished who has trampled the Son of God under foot, who has treated as an unholy thing the blood of the covenant that sanctified him, and who has insulted the Spirit of grace? [30]For we know him who said, "It is mine to avenge; I will repay," and again, "The Lord will judge his people." [31]It is a dreadful thing to fall into the hands of the living God.

1. *Why should Christians meet together? Is this the purpose of the Christian meetings you have experienced?*

2. *What does it mean to insult the Spirit of grace? How would one do this?*

3. *After strong words of assurance, that we can draw near to God, why does Hebrews have such a frightening warning of judgment?*

Day Five Reading and Questions:

Go back and read the entire passage.

1. *Notice how many times this passage says "once" or "once for all." Why is this repeated?*

2. *Are you confident that the sacrifice of Jesus forgives you? What boosts that confidence? What threatens that confidence?*

3. *If our hearts have been cleansed from a guilty conscience, should we never feel guilty? What is the place of guilt in the life of a Christian?*

MEDITATION ON HEBREWS 10:1-31

Do you feel near to God? Or do you sometimes feel far away? I must admit at times I feel near and at times I feel far.

When do we feel far away from God? Usually when we are most conscious of our sinfulness, when we take a good look at ourselves. Much of the time we can fool ourselves into thinking we are pretty good people, better than most. But then we crash head-on into reality. We lose our temper, betray those we love, and live out our selfish desires. It is then we feel far away from God.

How can we draw near to God when we are sinful? We can't. But we can draw near when we trust He has taken away our sins. Once for all. Forever. By his sacrifice Jesus has made us perfect forever. Forgiven forever. Holy forever.

All he asks is that we trust his forgiveness. If we do, then we come before God with complete confidence, not confidence in ourselves but in Jesus.

This is the amazing Spirit of grace that God gives us in Christ. All we must do is accept it. However, if we will not, if instead we wallow in our sinfulness and selfishness, then we insult the Spirit of grace, trample the Son of God underfoot, and reject the blood that bought us.

The choice is ours. We cannot choose to make ourselves worthy enough to come into God's presence. We can choose to trust that Jesus makes us worthy. Draw near to God!

"Father, you have sacrificed your Son, you have given us your Spirit of grace, you have forgiven us once for all. Lord may we joyfully embrace your holiness and draw near."

CONFIDENCE

(Hebrews 10:32-11:16)

Day One Reading and Questions:

[32]Remember those earlier days after you had received the light, when you stood your ground in a great contest in the face of suffering. [33]Sometimes you were publicly exposed to insult and persecution; at other times you stood side by side with those who were so treated. [34]You sympathized with those in prison and joyfully accepted the confiscation of your property, because you knew that you yourselves had better and lasting possessions.

[35]So do not throw away your confidence; it will be richly rewarded. [36]You need to persevere so that when you have done the will of God, you will receive what he has promised. [37]For in just a very little while,

"He who is coming will come and will not delay.

[38]But my righteous one will live by faith.

And if he shrinks back,

I will not be pleased with him."

[39]But we are not of those who shrink back and are destroyed, but of those who believe and are saved.

1. How do we respond to those who insult us because of our faith? How should we respond?

2. Why is perseverance so important for Christians? Why is it so difficult?

3. What does it mean to shrink back? Why might we be tempted to do this?

Day Two Reading and Questions:

[1]Now faith is being sure of what we hope for and certain of what we do not see. [2]This is what the ancients were commended for.

[3]By faith we understand that the universe was formed at God's command, so that what is seen was not made out of what was visible. [4]By faith Abel offered God a better sacrifice than Cain did. By faith he was commended as a righteous man, when God spoke well of his offerings. And by faith he still speaks, even though he is dead.

[5]By faith Enoch was taken from this life, so that he did not experience death; he could not be found, because God had taken him away. For before he was taken, he was commended as one who pleased God. [6]And without faith it is impossible to please God, because anyone who comes to him must believe that he exists and that he rewards those who earnestly seek him.

1. What is it we hope for but do not see? How does faith make that hope certain?

2. Can we prove God made the world or is it a matter of faith? Why?

3. What happened to faithful Abel? What happened to faithful Enoch? Does faith bring immediate rewards?

Day Three Reading and Questions:

[7]By faith Noah, when warned about things not yet seen, in holy fear built an ark to save his family. By his faith he condemned the world and became heir of the righteousness that comes by faith.

[8]By faith Abraham, when called to go to a place he would later receive as his inheritance, obeyed and went, even though he did not know where he was going. [9]By faith he made his home in the promised land like a stranger in a foreign country; he lived in tents, as did Isaac and Jacob, who were heirs with him of the same promise. [10]For he was looking forward to the city with foundations, whose architect and builder is God.

[11]By faith Abraham, even though he was past age—and Sarah herself was barren—was enabled to become a father because he considered him faithful who had made the promise. [12]And so from this one man, and he as good as dead, came descendants as numerous as the stars in the sky and as countless as the sand on the seashore.

1. What did Noah have to believe? Why was that hard?

2. Do you ever feel like Abraham, that you don't know where you are going? How should we live in light of that feeling?

3. Abraham believed the impossible, that he would have a child in his old age. What promise of God do you have difficulty believing because it seems impossible?

Day Four Reading and Questions:

[13]All these people were still living by faith when they died. They did not receive the things promised; they only saw them and welcomed them from a distance. And they admitted that they were aliens and strangers on earth. [14]People who say such things show that they are looking for a country of their own. [15]If they had been thinking of the country they had left, they would have had opportunity to return. [16]Instead, they were longing for a better country—a heavenly one. Therefore God is not ashamed to be called their God, for he has prepared a city for them.

1. *How did these people (and how can we) keep their faith when they did not receive what was promised them? Were they foolish to keep their faith?*

2. *How are we aliens and strangers on the earth?*

3. *How does looking forward to a better city and country help us live now?*

Day Five Reading and Questions:

Go back and read the entire passage.

1. *How does trust relate to being mistreated?*

2. *Who in this passage was immediately rewarded for faith? Who had to wait to receive what was promised? Why should we wait?*

3. What is harder to believe, that God exists or that he rewards those who seek him? Why?

MEDITATION ON HEBREWS 10:32-11:16

Sure. Certain. Confident.

Perhaps we feel like this often. Perhaps rarely.

Do we feel that way about our relationship to God? What gives us confidence before God? Are we confident because we are obedient? But we don't always obey. Are we confident because we see God's blessings? Then what happens when defeat and tragedy strike?

It is trust that makes us confident before God. Trust assures us of our hope. We trust that God rewards us for seeking him. We trust even when (especially when) reward does not come.

Abel trusts God and is murdered. Enoch trusts God and never dies. Noah believes in a flood like no one had ever seen. Abraham believes in a land of promise, a land he never gets in his lifetime. He believes he will have a child when he's near a hundred years old.

Sometimes God's people trust him and he delivers. Sometimes they trust him and they die as strangers and foreigners in the land of promise.

How can we be confident when trouble comes? When people mistreat us? We continue to trust. We persevere in faith, believing that God will keep his promises if only we wait for them. Wait just a little while longer.

"Father God, we wait for your promises, but for now they do not come. Increase our faith! Give us patient endurance! May we be faithful as those in the past have been."

LIVING BY FAITH

(Hebrews 11:17-12:3)

Day One Reading and Questions:

[17]By faith Abraham, when God tested him, offered Isaac as a sacrifice. He who had received the promises was about to sacrifice his one and only son, [18]even though God had said to him, "It is through Isaac that your offspring will be reckoned." [19]Abraham reasoned that God could raise the dead, and figuratively speaking, he did receive Isaac back from death.

[20]By faith Isaac blessed Jacob and Esau in regard to their future.

[21]By faith Jacob, when he was dying, blessed each of Joseph's sons, and worshiped as he leaned on the top of his staff.

[22]By faith Joseph, when his end was near, spoke about the exodus of the Israelites from Egypt and gave instructions about his bones.

1. Would you offer your child as a sacrifice if God told you to?

2. Does Abraham's faith make sense?

3. Why does it take faith to bless future generations?

Day Two Reading and Questions:

²³By faith Moses' parents hid him for three months after he was born, because they saw he was no ordinary child, and they were not afraid of the king's edict.

²⁴By faith Moses, when he had grown up, refused to be known as the son of Pharaoh's daughter. ²⁵He chose to be mistreated along with the people of God rather than to enjoy the pleasures of sin for a short time. ²⁶He regarded disgrace for the sake of Christ as of greater value than the treasures of Egypt, because he was looking ahead to his reward. ²⁷By faith he left Egypt, not fearing the king's anger; he persevered because he saw him who is invisible. ²⁸By faith he kept the Passover and the sprinkling of blood, so that the destroyer of the first-born would not touch the firstborn of Israel.

²⁹By faith the people passed through the Red Sea as on dry land; but when the Egyptians tried to do so, they were drowned.

³⁰By faith the walls of Jericho fell, after the people had marched around them for seven days.

³¹By faith the prostitute Rahab, because she welcomed the spies, was not killed with those who were disobedient.

1. *Why did it take faith to hide Moses? Did his parents act from faith or fear?*

2. *How did Moses see him who is invisible? How do we see him?*

3. *Why is Rahab an unusual example of faith?*

Day Three Reading and Questions:

[32]And what more shall I say? I do not have time to tell about Gideon, Barak, Samson, Jephthah, David, Samuel and the prophets, [33]who through faith conquered kingdoms, administered justice, and gained what was promised; who shut the mouths of lions, [34]quenched the fury of the flames, and escaped the edge of the sword; whose weakness was turned to strength; and who became powerful in battle and routed foreign armies. [35]Women received back their dead, raised to life again. Others were tortured and refused to be released, so that they might gain a better resurrection. [36]Some faced jeers and flogging, while still others were chained and put in prison. [37]They were stoned; they were sawed in two; they were put to death by the sword. They went about in sheepskins and goatskins, destitute, persecuted and mistreated— [38]the world was not worthy of them. They wandered in deserts and mountains, and in caves and holes in the ground.

[39]These were all commended for their faith, yet none of them received what had been promised. [40]God had planned something better for us so that only together with us would they be made perfect.

1. What great things did some accomplish by faith?

2. What terrible things did some suffer because of their faith?

3. Why does it say that none received what had been promised? Did not some receive it?

Day Four Reading and Questions:

[1]Therefore, since we are surrounded by such a great cloud of witnesses, let us throw off everything that hinders and the sin that

so easily entangles, and let us run with perseverance the race marked out for us. [2]Let us fix our eyes on Jesus, the author and perfecter of our faith, who for the joy set before him endured the cross, scorning its shame, and sat down at the right hand of the throne of God. [3]Consider him who endured such opposition from sinful men, so that you will not grow weary and lose heart.

1. *Who is the cloud of witnesses that surrounds us? How does that make you feel?*

2. *How do we fix our eyes on Jesus?*

3. *What was the joy set before Jesus? What joy is set before us?*

Day Five Reading and Questions:

Go back and read the entire passage.

1. *What makes you grow weary and lose heart as a Christian? How can we keep from losing heart?*

2. *Who is the real hero of all the biblical stories in this section?*

3. *Did Jesus have to have faith? Didn't he have sight of God?*

MEDITATION ON HEBREWS 11:17-12:3

Believing into the future. Trusting even in the face of death. Continuing the race when all is lost. Keeping on when it makes no sense keeping on.

This is what we are called to do as Christians. How can we do it? Who is strong enough for this? How can we possibly keep from growing tired and losing heart?

By looking at those who finished the race. Abraham, Isaac, Jacob, Joseph, Moses, Rahab, and countless others. All continued to trust God in the face of death. All looked to God's promise in the future, after their lifetimes. All withstood opposition and struggle and still remained faithful. All of them now stand on the sidelines and cheer us on, "We made it, so can you."

How can we be faithful when it seems all is lost? By looking at Jesus. Fixing our eyes on him. He too faced death, even death on the cross. He too had to trust that death, shame, and defeat were not the last words. He believed God would raise him from the dead. In the middle of agony, he knew there was joy before him.

We do not hang on literal crosses, but we do grow tired and discouraged. But no opposition should keep us from trusting the One who gave his own Son for us.

"God of love, when we cannot see where our lives are headed then fix our eyes on Jesus. Give us endurance in the race of life. Remind us of the joy before us."

DISCIPLINED HOLINESS

(Hebrews 12:4-29)

Day One Reading and Questions:

[4]In your struggle against sin, you have not yet resisted to the point of shedding your blood. [5]And you have forgotten that word of encouragement that addresses you as sons:

"My son, do not make light of the Lord's discipline,

and do not lose heart when he rebukes you,

[6]because the Lord disciplines those he loves,

and he punishes everyone he accepts as a son."

[7]Endure hardship as discipline; God is treating you as sons. For what son is not disciplined by his father? [8]If you are not disciplined (and everyone undergoes discipline), then you are illegitimate children and not true sons. [9]Moreover, we have all had human fathers who disciplined us and we respected them for it. How much more should we submit to the Father of our spirits and live! [10]Our fathers disciplined us for a little while as they thought best; but God disciplines us for our good, that we may share in his holiness. [11]No discipline seems pleasant at the time, but painful. Later on, however, it produces a harvest of righteousness and peace for those who have been trained by it.

[12]Therefore, strengthen your feeble arms and weak knees. [13]"Make level paths for your feet," so that the lame may not be disabled, but rather healed.

1. How is discipline a "word of encouragement"?

2. Why does God discipline us?

3. How does discipline lead to endurance in our Christian walk?

Day Two Reading and Questions:

[14]Make every effort to live in peace with all men and to be holy; without holiness no one will see the Lord. [15]See to it that no one misses the grace of God and that no bitter root grows up to cause trouble and defile many. [16]See that no one is sexually immoral, or is godless like Esau, who for a single meal sold his inheritance rights as the oldest son. [17]Afterward, as you know, when he wanted to inherit this blessing, he was rejected. He could bring about no change of mind, though he sought the blessing with tears.

1. What is holiness? How do we become holy?

2. How can we miss the grace of God?

3. How is Esau an example to us?

Day Three Reading and Questions:

[18]You have not come to a mountain that can be touched and that is burning with fire; to darkness, gloom and storm; [19]to a trumpet blast or to such a voice speaking words that those who heard it begged that no further word be spoken to them, [20]because they could not bear what was commanded: "If even an animal touches the mountain, it

must be stoned." [21]The sight was so terrifying that Moses said, "I am trembling with fear."

[22]But you have come to Mount Zion, to the heavenly Jerusalem, the city of the living God. You have come to thousands upon thousands of angels in joyful assembly, [23]to the church of the firstborn, whose names are written in heaven. You have come to God, the judge of all men, to the spirits of righteous men made perfect, [24]to Jesus the mediator of a new covenant, and to the sprinkled blood that speaks a better word than the blood of Abel.

1. *What is the first mountain described here? What is the contrast between it and Mount Zion?*

2. *How do we share the joy of the angels?*

3. *What does it mean to be part of the church of the firstborn? What did the firstborn receive in Bible times?*

Day Four Reading and Questions:

[25]See to it that you do not refuse him who speaks. If they did not escape when they refused him who warned them on earth, how much less will we, if we turn away from him who warns us from heaven? [26]At that time his voice shook the earth, but now he has promised, "Once more I will shake not only the earth but also the heavens."[27]The words "once more" indicate the removing of what can be shaken— that is, created things—so that what cannot be shaken may remain.

[28]Therefore, since we are receiving a kingdom that cannot be shaken, let us be thankful, and so worship God acceptably with reverence and awe, [29]for our "God is a consuming fire."

1. What warning does God give from heaven? Is it kind to warn others?

2. How is the kingdom one that cannot be shaken? What is the point of all the shaking language here?

3. "Our God is a consuming fire." Is this an encouraging word? A frightening word? Should we ever be frightened of God?

Day Five Reading and Questions:

Go back and read the entire passage.

1. How are discipline and holiness related?

2. How do the two mountains, Sinai and Zion, relate to discipline and holiness?

3. What does it look like to worship with reverence and awe?

MEDITATION ON HEBREWS 12:14-29

Among my many faults is this: I am easily discouraged. If something comes easy, I continue to do it. If it's difficult, I generally give up after a few tries.

Discipline is not my strong suit. Yet almost everything worthwhile is accomplished through discipline. Especially following Jesus.

It is hard to follow Jesus. That hardship sometimes takes the form of opposition from others. Most often, it takes the form of discouragement. Today looks a lot like yesterday. Tomorrow will look at lot like today. We grow tired of the same old thing. The road of holiness is long and our legs grow weary.

What we need is discipline. We need to see our hardships as evidence of God's love and signs of our legitimacy as children of God. We also need to see more clearly where the road of holiness leads. We do not approach a mountain of fear but a mountain of joy. Yes, that joy leads to reverence and awe but not to fear of punishment. For we come to a Savior who gave his blood for us.

Yes, we serve a powerful, holy God who calls us to be his children. Hearing that call, we approach him in confidence and with discipline. Discipline is no fun, but we need it. We continue to run our race with patience, even when it hurts. We do not lose heart for we know we run with a loving Savior toward a welcoming Father. No matter what, our faith will not be shaken.

"Father, give us discipline. Strengthen our hearts. Make us stronger through hardships. May we continue to follow Jesus through pain and through boredom."

LIVE AS OUTSIDERS
(Hebrews 13:1-25)

DAY ONE READING AND QUESTIONS:

[1]Keep on loving each other as brothers. [2]Do not forget to entertain strangers, for by so doing some people have entertained angels without knowing it. [3]Remember those in prison as if you were their fellow prisoners, and those who are mistreated as if you yourselves were suffering.

[4]Marriage should be honored by all, and the marriage bed kept pure, for God will judge the adulterer and all the sexually immoral.

1. *What is a biblical example of entertaining angels without knowing it? Do we still entertain angels today?*

2. *Should we care for all prisoners or are these particular prisoners, Christians who are persecuted?*

3. *How are loving our brothers, entertaining strangers, remembering prisoners, and being faithful in marriage all related?*

Day Two Reading and Questions:

[5]Keep your lives free from the love of money and be content with what you have, because God has said,

"Never will I leave you;

never will I forsake you."

[6]So we say with confidence,

"The Lord is my helper; I will not be afraid.

What can man do to me?"

[7]Remember your leaders, who spoke the word of God to you. Consider the outcome of their way of life and imitate their faith. [8]Jesus Christ is the same yesterday and today and forever.

[9]Do not be carried away by all kinds of strange teachings. It is good for our hearts to be strengthened by grace, not by ceremonial foods, which are of no value to those who eat them. [10]We have an altar from which those who minister at the tabernacle have no right to eat.

1. *Can we really be content with what we have? What would that look like?*

2. *What does contentment have to do with God's promise to never forsake us? How does contentment relate to fear?*

3. *Why is it comforting that Jesus is always the same? What does this have to do with remembering leaders who have gone before us? What does it have to do with avoiding strange teachings?*

Day Three Reading and Questions:

[11]The high priest carries the blood of animals into the Most Holy Place as a sin offering, but the bodies are burned outside the

camp. [12]And so Jesus also suffered outside the city gate to make the people holy through his own blood. [13]Let us, then, go to him outside the camp, bearing the disgrace he bore. [14]For here we do not have an enduring city, but we are looking for the city that is to come.

[15]Through Jesus, therefore, let us continually offer to God a sacrifice of praise—the fruit of lips that confess his name. [16]And do not forget to do good and to share with others, for with such sacrifices God is pleased.

[17]Obey your leaders and submit to their authority. They keep watch over you as men who must give an account. Obey them so that their work will be a joy, not a burden, for that would be of no advantage to you.

1. *What is the significance of following Jesus outside the camp? Do you feel like an outsider as a Christian? How?*

2. *What are the two sacrifices we make to God? Do churches tend to emphasize one of these over another? Why?*

3. *Are there limits to the obedience we give our leaders? Do you react negatively to the idea of obeying them? Why?*

Day Four Reading and Questions:

[18]Pray for us. We are sure that we have a clear conscience and desire to live honorably in every way. [19]I particularly urge you to pray so that I may be restored to you soon.

[20]May the God of peace, who through the blood of the eternal covenant brought back from the dead our Lord Jesus, that great Shepherd of the sheep, [21]equip you with everything good for doing his will, and may he work in us what is pleasing to him, through Jesus

Christ, to whom be glory for ever and ever. Amen.

[22]Brothers, I urge you to bear with my word of exhortation, for I have written you only a short letter.

[23]I want you to know that our brother Timothy has been released. If he arrives soon, I will come with him to see you.

[24]Greet all your leaders and all God's people. Those from Italy send you their greetings.

[25]Grace be with you all.

1. Why does the writer assure his readers of his honorable intentions?

2. If God equips us for doing good and works in us, what part do we have in doing what is pleasing to him?

3. How is Hebrews a word of exhortation or encouragement?

Day Five Reading and Questions:

Go back and read the entire passage.

1. This chapter touches on many subjects. Do you see an overall theme for the chapter?

2. What should be the relationship between leaders and the church they lead? What makes this difficult?

3. What does Jesus do for us according to this chapter?

MEDITATION ON HEBREWS 13:1-25

Outsiders. No one wants to be an outsider. Rejected. Scorned. Shamed.

Yet that is precisely what Jesus calls us to be. He calls us to follow him outside the camp, outside the city. There we experience the disgrace he did at his crucifixion.

What does it mean to be an outsider? How does one live outside the camp? What does life look like when it challenges the accepted norms of our culture?

It looks live love. Love for our brothers and sisters. Love for the stranger. Committed love between husbands and wives. This kind of love, costly love that is not always best for us but is best for others, this love challenges the ways of our culture. It is not the love known inside the city, the camp, the world in which we live. It is a supernatural love from God himself through Christ, a love that always gives.

What makes us outsiders? Our attitude toward money. In a world where too much is never enough, we are content with what we have. We trust God, not money, to protect and help us.

In a world where freedom and choice are prized, we honor and submit to our leaders, knowing that they watch out for us. In a time of self-reliance, we depend on the great Shepherd.

No wonder those who received this letter faced persecution. They were a threat to the status quo. Hebrews encourages us boldly to go to Jesus outside the camp, to embrace our identity as outsiders, and to show love to both insiders and outsiders. This is the way of Jesus.

"Jesus, our Shepherd, lead us as your flock outside the camp. Give us the courage to suffer in love as outsiders, as you suffered in shame for us."

JAMES: THE WISDOM OF JESUS

THE SPIRITUALITY OF JAMES

Some, like Martin Luther, have found little of spiritual value in James, misunderstanding it as a legalistic book. Others prize it as a practical guide to Christianity, but not as deeply spiritual. That too is a misunderstanding. Reading through James you will discover that it is a guide to a spirituality from above, even though James never specifically mentions the Holy Spirit.

WISDOM SPIRITUALITY

Wisdom is one gift needed by Christians throughout the ages. It is particularly needed in our time, when the forces of secularization and worldliness threaten the church. We need wisdom to view the trials of this age as pure joy. Such wisdom does not come naturally from our own abilities and efforts. It is God's gift alone. We should pray regularly for this wisdom, trusting that God will freely give it to guide his people (James 1:5-7). All our prayers should go to God with confidence not doubt.

But James speaks of two contrasting "wisdoms," contrasting true, meek wisdom that comes from God with a so-called "wisdom" that is worldly, focused solely on this life. The argument here is similar to his argument on the two types of faith (2:14-26). Faith without deeds is dead. It is no faith at all. So a wisdom that is not humble is really no wisdom at all. Such wisdom springs not from humility before God and meekness before neighbor but from bitter envy and selfish ambition (James 3:13-18).

Moral Spirituality

Some forms of spirituality are so personal and private that they neglect moral action. Not so biblical spirituality. In James, faith and works always belong together. Thus James is primarily ethical instruction. The Greek philosophers gave such moral instruction in the ancient world. Proverbs is an Old Testament book of morals. Even earlier, Leviticus gives moral instruction to Israel, especially in the "Holiness Code" of Leviticus 19. James often refers to that chapter in his book.

More significantly, James can best be thought of as a commentary on the Sermon on the Mount. If the Sermon is the wisdom of Jesus, then James takes that wisdom and applies it to a new generation. This in no way makes James a legalist, but one who serves the church by calling it back to what Jesus intended it to be, a community that practices a higher righteousness (Matthew 5:20). For James and for Jesus, genuine spirituality is shown by concrete acts of compassion for those in need (James 1:27; 2:15-16).

"Impractical" Spirituality

Some would say James gives a practical spirituality, dealing with people where they are and giving specific steps on how they can improve. Of course, James is practical if one means he is concerned with Christian living. His words are certainly relevant to contemporary Christians.

However, by calling James "practical" some mean it simply enforces our own cultural values. Such could not be farther from the truth. James is a thoroughly impractical book in that he challenges our assumptions at every turn. Like Job and Ecclesiastes, he condemns human wisdom and is pessimistic of the ability of humans to reform themselves. He is hopeful, however, of God's transcendent power in the believer. By calling on his readers to receive "wisdom from above" (James 3:17), he fights worldliness in the church by calling Christians to wait patiently for the Lord's return. If we feel comfortable with the teaching of James (or rather, with the teaching of Jesus, since he is the original source of James's teaching), then we have probably misunderstood it. It is a radical, counter-cultural message that the church today needs to hear and do.

MEDITATIONS

TESTED

(James 1:1-27)

Day One Reading and Questions:

[1]James, a servant of God and of the Lord Jesus Christ,

To the twelve tribes scattered among the nations:

Greetings.

[2]Consider it pure joy, my brothers, whenever you face trials of many kinds, [3]because you know that the testing of your faith develops perseverance. [4]Perseverance must finish its work so that you may be mature and complete, not lacking anything. [5]If any of you lacks wisdom, he should ask God, who gives generously to all without finding fault, and it will be given to him. [6]But when he asks, he must believe and not doubt, because he who doubts is like a wave of the sea, blown and tossed by the wind. [7]That man should not think he will receive anything from the Lord; [8]he is a double-minded man, unstable in all he does.

1. Do we ever associate trials with joy? How can trials produce joy?

2. What is wisdom? How do we get it?

3. What does it mean to be double-minded? How does that relate to asking for wisdom?

Day Two Reading and Questions:

[9]The brother in humble circumstances ought to take pride in his high position. [10]But the one who is rich should take pride in his low position, because he will pass away like a wild flower. [11]For the sun rises with scorching heat and withers the plant; its blossom falls and its beauty is destroyed. In the same way, the rich man will fade away even while he goes about his business.

1. What kind of pride should the poor (those in humble circumstances) have? How do they have a high position?

2. How do the rich have a low position?

3. Is this the way we usually think of rich and poor?

Day Three Reading and Questions:

[12]Blessed is the man who perseveres under trial, because when he has stood the test, he will receive the crown of life that God has promised to those who love him.
[13]When tempted, no one should say, "God is tempting me." For God cannot be tempted by evil, nor does he tempt anyone; [14]but each one is tempted when, by his own evil desire, he is dragged away and

enticed. [15]Then, after desire has conceived, it gives birth to sin; and sin, when it is full-grown, gives birth to death.

[16]Don't be deceived, my dear brothers. [17]Every good and perfect gift is from above, coming down from the Father of the heavenly lights, who does not change like shifting shadows. [18]He chose to give us birth through the word of truth, that we might be a kind of first-fruits of all he created.

1. Why is it important that God does not tempt us?

2. How is sin a process? How does it help us to understand that process?

3. Why is it important that the Father does not change? How does this help us when we are tempted?

Day Four Reading and Questions:

[19]My dear brothers, take note of this: Everyone should be quick to listen, slow to speak and slow to become angry, [20]for man's anger does not bring about the righteous life that God desires. [21]Therefore, get rid of all moral filth and the evil that is so prevalent and humbly accept the word planted in you, which can save you.

[22]Do not merely listen to the word, and so deceive yourselves. Do what it says. [23]Anyone who listens to the word but does not do what it says is like a man who looks at his face in a mirror [24]and, after looking at himself, goes away and immediately forgets what he looks like. [25]But the man who looks intently into the perfect law that gives freedom, and continues to do this, not forgetting what he has heard, but doing it—he will be blessed in what he does.

[26]If anyone considers himself religious and yet does not keep a tight rein on his tongue, he deceives himself and his religion is worth-

less. [27]Religion that God our Father accepts as pure and faultless is this: to look after orphans and widows in their distress and to keep oneself from being polluted by the world.

1. *Why are most of us quicker to speak than to listen? What can we do about it? How does this tendency relate to anger?*

2. *What is the point of the mirror illustration?*

3. *Are caring for the needy and not being polluted by the world related? How?*

DAY FIVE READING AND QUESTIONS:

1. *How are we tested by life in the following areas: Difficulties? Money? Speech? Caring for the needy?*

2. *When do we particularly need wisdom? How can we get it?*

3. *How does God plant his word in us? How does that word save us?*

MEDITATION ON JAMES 1:1-27

As a student, I hated tests. Having taught for almost thirty years, I've given hundreds of tests.

Am I a hypocrite? I hate tests but I give them. Am I mean to my students? If I care for them, should I plague them with tests?

I test because I care. I test because I want them to learn.

That's the difference between a test and a temptation. God

tests our faith because he wants us to learn and grow. Satan tempts us through our own desires because he wants us to fail. God never tempts. He only gives good gifts. He is consistent in his giving.

So the same trial can be a test or a temptation. A test if we pass. A temptation if we fail. But how do we overcome temptation?

Through wisdom. Wisdom is being skilled at living life. Such wisdom is not merely natural but is a gift from God. A gift he gives to us if we only ask.

God's gift of wisdom can keep us from the lure of wealth. It can cause us to open our ears and close our mouths. It creates true religion where we care for those in need and stand against the ways of the world.

Boy, how we need wisdom. All we need to do is ask.

"Father, in full assurance we ask for your wisdom today. Keep us from divided hearts and minds. May we trust fully in your goodness."

ACTIVE MERCY

(James 2:1-26)

DAY ONE READING AND QUESTIONS:

[1]My brothers, as believers in our glorious Lord Jesus Christ, don't show favoritism. [2]Suppose a man comes into your meeting wearing a gold ring and fine clothes, and a poor man in shabby clothes also comes in. [3]If you show special attention to the man wearing fine clothes and say, "Here's a good seat for you," but say to the poor man, "You stand there" or "Sit on the floor by my feet," [4]have you not discriminated among yourselves and become judges with evil thoughts?

[5]Listen, my dear brothers: Has not God chosen those who are poor in the eyes of the world to be rich in faith and to inherit the kingdom he promised those who love him? [6]But you have insulted the poor. Is it not the rich who are exploiting you? Are they not the ones who are dragging you into court? [7]Are they not the ones who are slandering the noble name of him to whom you belong?

1. What is favoritism? Why might we favor the rich over the poor?

2. Have you ever seen favoritism in the church? What form did it take?

3. Does God favor the poor according to this passage? Why or why not?

Day Two Reading and Questions:

[8]If you really keep the royal law found in Scripture, "Love your neighbor as yourself," you are doing right. [9]But if you show favoritism, you sin and are convicted by the law as lawbreakers. [10]For whoever keeps the whole law and yet stumbles at just one point is guilty of breaking all of it. [11]For he who said, "Do not commit adultery," also said, "Do not murder." If you do not commit adultery but do commit murder, you have become a lawbreaker.

[12]Speak and act as those who are going to be judged by the law that gives freedom, [13]because judgment without mercy will be shown to anyone who has not been merciful. Mercy triumphs over judgment!

1. What is the royal law? Why is it called "royal"?

2. How does the law give freedom? What law is he talking about?

3. Give specific examples of times you have needed mercy from God and from others. Do we give the same mercy to others? Do we show mercy to those who are discriminated against by others?

Day Three Reading and Questions:

[14]What good is it, my brothers, if a man claims to have faith but has no deeds? Can such faith save him? [15]Suppose a brother or sister is without clothes and daily food. [16]If one of you says to him, "Go, I wish you well; keep warm and well fed," but does nothing about his physical needs, what good is it? [17]In the same way, faith by itself, if is not accompanied by action, is dead.

[18]But someone will say, "You have faith; I have deeds."

Show me your faith without deeds, and I will show you my faith by what I do.

[19]You believe that there is one God. Good! Even the demons believe that—and shudder.

1. What specific deeds or acts of faith are mentioned here?

2. How do we show we have faith?

3. What do demons believe about God? Do demons have saving faith? Why is it not enough to believe in God?

Day Four Reading and Questions:

[20]You foolish man, do you want evidence that faith without deeds is useless? [21]Was not our ancestor Abraham considered righteous for what he did when he offered his son Isaac on the altar? [22]You see that his faith and his actions were working together, and his faith was made complete by what he did. [23]And the scripture was fulfilled that says, "Abraham believed God, and it was credited to him as righteousness," and he was called God's friend. [24]You see that a person is justified by what he does and not by faith alone.

[25]In the same way, was not even Rahab the prostitute considered righteous for what she did when she gave lodging to the spies and sent them off in a different direction? [26]As the body without the spirit is dead, so faith without deeds is dead.

1. How did Abraham show his faith? Do we have that much faith?

2. Do our good deeds save or justify us? What does it mean that we are not justified by faith alone?

3. Why do you think Rahab is given as an example here, alongside of Abraham?

DAY FIVE READING AND QUESTIONS:

Go back and read the entire passage.

1. What does it mean to love our neighbor? How do we show that love?

2. Is there a contradiction between Paul who says one is saved by faith without works (see Romans 3:27-4:3) and James who clearly says faith without works cannot save?

3. How does showing mercy relate to an active faith?

MEDITATION ON JAMES 2:1-26

Are you ever tempted to do the right thing? You know how it is. You see the fellow with sign on the side of the road, "Will work for food." Or you see the woman with a child holding out her cup on the street and asking for spare change. You feel for them. You want their lives to be better. But you're in a hurry, and there are too many asking for help, and what good would a few dollars do them.

But you feel genuine compassion for them.

No you don't. James makes it clear that true compassion is not a feeling but an action. If you only feel for them, what good does that do them?

So what would be the right thing to do? Do we always give money? Does that always help? Do we find a job for them? Take them to the social services office? Bring them into our homes? Feed them from the church pantry?

I don't know. We don't always know how best to help those in need. But one thing is for sure, we must do something for them. Otherwise, our "faith" is a sham. What we must not do is feel sorry for them and move on. What we must not do is to judge others by their outward appearance.

To claim faith is to claim relation to God. And our God shows no favoritism. He chooses the poor to be rich in faith. He not only feels sorry for us, but he does something. He gives his own Son for us.

Such giving love is the law of the King, the royal law. Love your neighbor as yourself. This is the law that judges us. We dare not love in word alone, but in action.

"God of love, your compassion is boundless. You show your love to us in countless ways. May we do more than speak your love. May we live it toward others this day."

HEART AND TONGUE

(James 3:1-4:3)

DAY ONE READING AND QUESTIONS:

¹Not many of you should presume to be teachers, my brothers, because you know that we who teach will be judged more strictly. ²We all stumble in many ways. If anyone is never at fault in what he says, he is a perfect man, able to keep his whole body in check.

³When we put bits into the mouths of horses to make them obey us, we can turn the whole animal. ⁴Or take ships as an example. Although they are so large and are driven by strong winds, they are steered by a very small rudder wherever the pilot wants to go. ⁵Likewise the tongue is a small part of the body, but it makes great boasts. Consider what a great forest is set on fire by a small spark. ⁶The tongue also is a fire, a world of evil among the parts of the body. It corrupts the whole person, sets the whole course of his life on fire, and is itself set on fire by hell.

1. *Why will teachers be judged more strictly?*

2. *How can the tongue control the whole shape of our lives?*

3. *Is the tongue evil in itself? What can make it evil?*

Day Two Reading and Questions:

[7]All kinds of animals, birds, reptiles and creatures of the sea are being tamed and have been tamed by man, [8]but no man can tame the tongue. It is a restless evil, full of deadly poison.

[9]With the tongue we praise our Lord and Father, and with it we curse men, who have been made in God's likeness. [10]Out of the same mouth come praise and cursing. My brothers, this should not be. [11]Can both fresh water and salt water flow from the same spring? [12]My brothers, can a fig tree bear olives, or a grapevine bear figs? Neither can a salt spring produce fresh water.

1. *If no one can tame the tongue, then why do we have these warnings about it? Can we do nothing to tame the tongue?*

2. *Why is inconsistency with the tongue such a problem? Why would those who praise God curse others?*

3. *What is the point of the water and produce illustrations?*

Day Three Reading and Questions:

[13]Who is wise and understanding among you? Let him show it by his good life, by deeds done in the humility that comes from wisdom. [14]But if you harbor bitter envy and selfish ambition in your hearts, do not boast about it or deny the truth. [15]Such "wisdom" does not come down from heaven but is earthly, unspiritual, of the devil. [16]For where you have envy and selfish ambition, there you find disorder and every evil practice.

[17]But the wisdom that comes from heaven is first of all pure; then peace-loving, considerate, submissive, full of mercy and good

fruit, impartial and sincere. [18]Peacemakers who sow in peace raise a harvest of righteousness.

1. How does one show wisdom? Is this similar to how one shows faith?

2. What characterizes earthly wisdom?

3. What things characterize wisdom from heaven?

DAY FOUR READING AND QUESTIONS:

[1]What causes fights and quarrels among you? Don't they come from your desires that battle within you? [2]You want something but don't get it. You kill and covet, but you cannot have what you want. You quarrel and fight. You do not have, because you do not ask God. [3]When you ask, you do not receive, because you ask with wrong motives, that you may spend what you get on your pleasures.

1. How does the worldly wisdom discussed above lead to fights and quarrels?

2. Can desires actually lead to murder? Give an example.

3. Should we ask God for anything we desire?

DAY FIVE READING AND QUESTIONS:

Go back and read the entire passage.

1. How does wisdom relate to controlling the tongue?

2. Is ambition a good thing or a bad thing?

3. Compare the description of wisdom in verses 17-18 with the fruit of the Spirit in Galatians 5:22-23. Are they similar? What might this say about the source of heavenly wisdom?

MEDITATION ON JAMES 3:1-4:3

"I regret saying that." It seems I have such regrets often. I don't think I am alone. Who among us has not desperately wanted to take back our words? But how can we control our tongues? Is it a just a matter of speaking less, or thinking before we speak? If so, why do we still regret what we say?

What is at stake here is not just watching our words but being controlled by God. As Jesus said, "For out of the overflow of the heart the mouth speaks" (Matthew 12:34b). What we need is not so much self-improvement but character. The real question is, "Who controls our speech?" or rather, "Who controls our life?" James reminds us that the true answer to this question is not seen in our intentions but in our speech and actions. It is a matter of the heart.

Or rather a matter of who controls our heart. Do we live according to worldly wisdom? What passes for wisdom or common sense in our world tells us that positive thinking, self-promotion, and tapping into hidden internal resources will bring happiness, excellence, and success. Such thinking is not just "out there" in the world; it is taken for granted in the church.

God offers us another type of wisdom, a heavenly common sense that is in direct opposition to the thinking of our age. This wisdom seeks peace, not success. It desires purity, not happiness. It shows itself in a willingness to yield to others, a sharp contrast to ambitious self-promotion.

Are we humble enough to receive this wisdom from God? If so, he will give it to us. And if we receive it, this heavenly wisdom will be shown even in our speech.

"Father, give us the wisdom from above. May your words be in our hearts and on our tongues, so we may be people of peace."

THE WORLD OR GOD?

(James 4:4-17)

DAY ONE READING AND QUESTIONS:

⁴You adulterous people, don't you know that friendship with the world is hatred toward God? Anyone who chooses to be a friend of the world becomes an enemy of God. ⁵Or do you think Scripture says without reason that the spirit he caused to live in us envies intensely? ⁶But he gives us more grace. That is why Scripture says:
"God opposes the proud
but gives grace to the humble."

1. Why does the writer use the word "adulterous" to describe the attitude here?

2. What does it mean to be a friend of the world? What are some ways we try to be friends of the world?

3. Does humility earn grace? Why do the humble receive more grace?

Day Two Reading and Questions:

[7]Submit yourselves, then, to God. Resist the devil, and he will flee from you. [8]Come near to God and he will come near to you. Wash your hands, you sinners, and purify your hearts, you double-minded. [9]Grieve, mourn and wail. Change your laughter to mourning and your joy to gloom. [10]Humble yourselves before the Lord, and he will lift you up.

1. *What are some ways we can resist the devil?*

2. *What does it mean to be double-minded? How do we prevent this?*

3. *Shouldn't Christians be joyful? Why are we told here to grieve, mourn, and wail? What are we to wail about?*

Day Three Reading and Questions:

[11]Brothers, do not slander one another. Anyone who speaks against his brother or judges him speaks against the law and judges it. When you judge the law, you are not keeping it, but sitting in judgment on it. [12]There is only one Lawgiver and Judge, the one who is able to save and destroy. But you—who are you to judge your neighbor?

1. *What is slander? How you ever been slandered? Have you ever slandered others?*

2. *How is speaking against a brother speaking against the law?*

3. *Should we never judge our neighbor? Can we never condemn the actions of another?*

Day Four Reading and Questions:

¹³Now listen, you who say, "Today or tomorrow we will go to this or that city, spend a year there, carry on business and make money." ¹⁴Why, you do not even know what will happen tomorrow. What is your life? You are a mist that appears for a little while and then vanishes. ¹⁵Instead, you ought to say, "If it is the Lord's will, we will live and do this or that." ¹⁶As it is, you boast and brag. All such boasting is evil. ¹⁷Anyone, then, who knows the good he ought to do and doesn't do it, sins.

1. *Shouldn't we make plans in our businesses and our lives? What's wrong with such planning?*

2. *Is life short, like a mist? If so, do we live as if it is short?*

3. *Is it enough to say, "If the Lord wills"? How would we live if we really meant that question?*

Day Five Reading and Questions:

Go back and read the entire passage.

1. *What comes to mind when you hear the word, "worldly"? Is slander worldly? Is making plans without God worldly?*

2. *Do you find it hard to submit to God? What does it mean to submit? Can we submit and still have things our way?*

3. *When we want to be successful in this world and still be right with God, is this not like adultery? How?*

MEDITATION ON JAMES 4:4-17

Worldly. What does it mean to be worldly? Some of us can remember a time when "worldly" meant drinking, smoking, dancing, and going to the movies. It didn't take much to be worldly when I was a kid!

But worldliness is much more subtle than that. To be a friend of the world, all it takes is to be mostly like all the "good" people around us. It means judging others by appearance. It means looking out for ourselves. It means putting other people down. It means making our plans for the future the way all families, businesses, and churches plan.

Such worldliness doesn't seem bad at all. "That's just the way things are," we say.

Precisely. But that's the problem. "The way things are" is not the way God wants things to be. Indeed, it is not really the way things are, but merely how we have been deceived into seeing them. Such worldliness is not God's way. And God's way is truly the way things are and (more importantly) the way things will be.

So if we are caught up in worldliness (and it takes no effort to be caught), what should we do? James is clear. We turn. Repent. Mourn. We humble ourselves before God, admitting we have tried to have both him and the world.

And God will lift us up.

"Father of mercy, have mercy on us as sinners. Purify our hearts. Cleanse our double-minds. Make us hungry for you alone, not for the deception of the world."

GOD OR MONEY?

(James 5:1-20)

DAY ONE READING AND QUESTIONS:

[1]Now listen, you rich people, weep and wail because of the misery that is coming upon you. [2]Your wealth has rotted, and moths have eaten your clothes. [3]Your gold and silver are corroded. Their corrosion will testify against you and eat your flesh like fire. You have hoarded wealth in the last days. [4]Look! The wages you failed to pay the workmen who mowed your fields are crying out against you. The cries of the harvesters have reached the ears of the Lord Almighty. [5]You have lived on earth in luxury and self-indulgence. You have fattened yourselves in the day of slaughter. [6]You have condemned and murdered innocent men, who were not opposing you.

1. *Are riches in themselves evil? What will wealth do for (or to) rich people in this passage?*

2. *How do the rich hurt others in this passage?*

3. *If riches are so harmful, why do we seek them?*

Day Two Reading and Questions:

[7]Be patient, then, brothers, until the Lord's coming. See how the farmer waits for the land to yield its valuable crop and how patient he is for the autumn and spring rains. [8]You too, be patient and stand firm, because the Lord's coming is near. [9]Don't grumble against each other, brothers, or you will be judged. The Judge is standing at the door! [10]Brothers, as an example of patience in the face of suffering, take the prophets who spoke in the name of the Lord. [11]As you know, we consider blessed those who have persevered. You have heard of Job's perseverance and have seen what the Lord finally brought about. The Lord is full of compassion and mercy.

1. How are farmers patient? How is this an example for Christians?

2. What does patience have to do with grumbling?

3. How were the prophets and Job patient? Did they never complain? What kind of patience did they have?

Day Three Reading and Questions:

[12]Above all, my brothers, do not swear—not by heaven or by earth or by anything else. Let your "Yes" be yes, and your "No," no, or you will be condemned.

[13]Is any one of you in trouble? He should pray. Is anyone happy? Let him sing songs of praise. [14]Is any one of you sick? He should call the elders of the church to pray over him and anoint him with oil in the name of the Lord. [15]And the prayer offered in faith will make the sick person well; the Lord will raise him up. If he has sinned, he will

be forgiven. [16]Therefore confess your sins to each other and pray for each other so that you may be healed. The prayer of a righteous man is powerful and effective.

1. *What is swearing? Why should we not swear?*

2. *What is the role of the oil in this passage? Does the oil heal? How is it related to prayer?*

3. *Do you have someone to whom you confess? Should you?*

DAY FOUR READING AND QUESTIONS:

[17]Elijah was a man just like us. He prayed earnestly that it would not rain, and it did not rain on the land for three and a half years. [18]Again he prayed, and the heavens gave rain, and the earth produced its crops.

[19]My brothers, if one of you should wander from the truth and someone should bring him back, [20]remember this: Whoever turns a sinner from the error of his way will save him from death and cover over a multitude of sins.

1. *Are the biblical heroes really like us?*

2. *Can we stop and start the rain by prayer?*

3. *Why is it important to bring a brother or sister back from sin? Why are we reluctant to confront others about their sins?*

Day Five Reading and Questions:

Go back and read the entire passage.

1. How should rich people respond to this passage? How should poor and oppressed people respond?

2. How are patience and prayer related?

3. Why do you think James ends so abruptly? Are the last two verses a good ending for the letter?

MEDITATION ON JAMES 5:1-20

God or money?

Most of the time, we fool ourselves into thinking we do not have to choose. We can have God and money.

But what is it that brings us security, meaning, and happiness? God or money? Do we rely on bank accounts, home equity, retirement plans, and insurance? Or do we trust in a God who saves his people?

Again we may answer, "both." But what do we do when we lose our job, the market tumbles, the bank repossesses our house, and the insurance policies are canceled? What do we do in the face of suffering? Trust our health plan? Rely on government safety nets? Or do we put our trust in a faithful God?

None of these things—savings, insurance, houses, jobs, and government programs—are wrong in themselves. But all are dangerous. They tempt us to rely on them, not God.

So what do we do when trouble strikes? We wait patiently. We pray in faith. We do not blame others and grumble against them. Instead we rely on our brothers and sisters. We ask for their prayers.

We confess. We confront them with their sins and they confront us with ours. All to turn us back to the path of truth.

God or money? The choice is ours.

"Father of all, may we rely on you, not on our wealth. May we bring justice and mercy to the poor, as you show mercy to those who wait and pray."

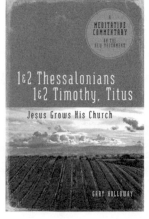

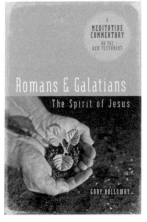
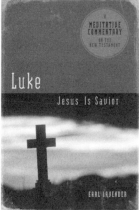